# The Family Legacy Journal

# THE Family *Legacy* Journal

MICHAEL TANNER

NASHVILLE

NEW YORK • LONDON • MELBOURNE • VANCOUVER

# The Family Legacy Journal



Published in New York, New York, by Morgan James Publishing. Morgan James is a trademark of Morgan James, LLC. www.MorganJamesPublishing.com



ISBN 9781683509240 paperback
ISBN 9781683509257 eBook
Library of Congress Control Number: 2017919487

**Cover Design & Interior Design by:**
Christopher Kirk
www.GFSstudio.com

# Dedication

Dedicated to my wonderful family.

Jennifer, Ensley, Jacob, and Noah, you deserve the best husband and father I can be. I would sacrifice my life for you. To prove it, I commit to live every day to serve you.

# SEVEN REASONS THIS JOURNAL WON'T FAIL YOU LIKE ALL THE REST.

1 **It's based on timeless biblical wisdom.** For the ardent believer in Jesus and the God of the Bible, that statement is sufficient. For the Bible skeptic, intellectual integrity requires you, at a minimum, acknowledge the incredible wisdom contained in the Bible. You can enjoy the benefits of journaling according to biblical wisdom without adopting a belief in the salvation described therein.

2 **It's based on science.** Lo and behold, science often supports the wisdom of the Bible. This journaling process is supported by science. Science has proven gratitude and positive thinking fosters a happier life. This journal guides you to that happier life.

3 **It isn't a blank journal.** This journal isn't just a book of blank pages. Too many of us get lost in a blank page. We don't have the natural abilities to organize our thoughts onto paper. The guidance provided in this journal allows you to focus on your thoughts rather than worry about organizing each page.

4 **It works for people who aren't writers.** This journal doesn't require you to be a writer. In fact, this journaling process doesn't even require that you write hundreds of words each day. The journal is more about getting your thoughts on paper rather than developing your personal memoir.

5 **It overcomes your lack of commitment or consistency.** Have you committed to journaling before, but failed to be consistent? The simple and consistent, yet beneficial, format of this journal reduces the writing burden that often trips up the most well-intended journalist.

6 **It provides guidance.** Did I mention this journal provides daily guidance along your journaling experience? While simple, the guidance provided in this journal brings about great positive impact in your life -- it's proven by the Bible and science.

7 **It provides an easy view of your history and growth.** Journaling isn't always about the here and now. Recounting our past helps us recognize how far we've come, how much we've grown, and how much we've endured. These retrospectives are crucial to future growth and made easy with the aid of this journal.

# HOW IT WORKS

## 1 Why a journal focused on family?

*"Whoever brings ruin on their family will inherit only wind, and the fool will be servant to the wise."*

**Proverbs 11:29 (NIV)**

The Bible offers significant wisdom regarding the family. This particular Proverb speaks to the importance of family and maintaining healthy relationships within the family.

The National Review cites three scientific studies that describe the benefits of strong family relationships. More specifically, the benefits are realized by those families adhering to a traditional definition of a family — married man and woman with children. While this study focused on economic and academic measures, there are countless other studies that highlight the social, mental, health, and spiritual benefits of family.

## 2 Gratitude

**I am thankful for...**

1) *the health of my children*
2) *the career that provides for my family*
3) *able to get up according to plan this morning*

**Today was a great day because...**

1) *my daughter responded to my text messages today*
2) *traffic was light today*
3) *able to have lunch with Gary today*

*"Don't worry about anything, but in everything, through prayer and petition with thanksgiving, let your requests be made known to God. And the peace of God, which surpasses every thought, will guard your hearts and minds in Christ Jesus."*

**Philippians 4:6-7 (HCSB)**

The Bible speaks of peace that surpasses all understanding comforting the heart of a person who prays and petitions God with gratitude.

Scientific studies have proven intentional gratitude to be a major factor in one's happiness and feeling better. Harvard Health Publications says, "Expressing thanks may be one of the simplest ways to feel better."

## 3 Reflection

**Scripture Reflection**

*This verse forces me to examine if I love my wife as myself. This verse also connects the word respect with the previous mentioned word submission.*

**Quote Reflection**

*Wow, living for my wife rather than myself, while very difficult, is the single most important thing I can do as a husband.*

**I could have made today better by…**

*taking sufficient time to calm down before reprimanding my son for his messy room*

*"Counsel in a man's heart is deep water; but a man of understanding draws it out."*

**Proverbs 20:5 (HCSB)**

The Bible speaks often about the need for reflection. Self-reflection and reflection upon God produces wisdom.

The Association for Psychological Science says, "mindful reflection is not just important in an academic context – it's also essential to our ability to make meaning of the world around us. Inward attention is an important contributor to the development of moral thinking and reasoning and is linked with overall socioemotional well-being."

# 4 Affirmation

**Affirmation --- I am ...**

Able to endure the tough schedule at work today

A better father than I give myself credit for

*"Set your minds on what is above, not on what is on the earth."*
**Colossians 3:2 (HCSB)**

Multiple times the Bible reminds us to focus our mind and thoughts on positive aspects and desires of life. Intentional affirmations create the needed mental focus for accomplishing our deepest desires.

Oxford Academic conducted brain imaging tests to study self-affirmations and conclude, "These neural correlates of self-affirmation were further associated with objectively measured behavior change, suggesting the external validity of the affirmation task. Taken together, our results highlight ways in which brain systems implicated in positive valuation and self-related processing may be reinforced by prospection and suggest novel insight into the balance of processes supporting affirmation." In layman's terms, Oxford Academic found that self-affirmations modify our behavior in objective and measurable ways.

# 5 Morning Routine

The morning routine is crucial to beginning a successful day. This is not to say the morning routine must start or end before a certain time. The power of the morning routine is simply found in starting your day with this journaling process. Whether your day begins a four in the morning or three in the afternoon, starting your day with this journaling process will bring about the desired benefits.

*"Very early in the morning, while it was still dark,*
*He got up, went out, and made His way to a deserted*
*place. And He was praying there."*
**Mark 1:35 (HCSB)**

Jesus considered his morning routine important and intentionally planned time early in the day for thanksgiving, reflection, affirmation, and prayer.

Countless books have been written regarding the morning routine of those deemed to be successful. In almost all cases, those morning routines include some aspect of meditation, self-reflection, and affirmation.

## 6 Evening Routine

The evening routine is also crucial to calming the mind and allowing appropriate rest. A great day tomorrow begins with proper preparation tonight. The evening routine is the proper setup for your best tomorrow possible.

*"I will both lie down and sleep in peace, for You alone, LORD, make me live in safety."*

**Psalms 4:8 (HCSB)**

God rested! Certainly if God needs to rest, so do we. This journaling process allows for the calming of the mind and reduction of stimulates, empowering one to experience deep rest and sleep.

Sleep scientist Patrick Fuller offers several tips for appropriate sleep and rest. He offers the tips of setting the sleeping mood and avoiding screens prior to bedtime. This journaling process allows for both. By allowing you to journal your final thoughts and reflections, the mind is cleared of thoughts that keep it spinning well into the night. Secondly, while writing in your journal, you are avoiding disruptive screen time prior to bedtime.

Date: 7 / 11 / 17

*However, let each one of you love his wife as himself,*
*and let the wife see that she respects her husband.*
**Ephesians 5:33 (ESV)**

**I am thankful for…**

1) the health of my children
2) the career that provides for my family
3) I was able to get up according to plan this morning

**Scripture Reflection**

This verse forces me to examine if I love my wife as myself. This verse also onnects the word "respect" with the previous mention word "submission."

**Affirmation — I am…**

able to endure the tough schedule at work today
a better father than I give myself credit for

**Personal Notes**

Lord, please don't let me mess this up today
I need to encourage Jennifer today

*"Whether we are husband or wife, we are not to live for ourselves but for the other. And that is the hardest yet single most important function of being a husband or a wife in marriage."*

**Timothy J. Keller**

**Quote Reflection**

Wow, living for my wife rather than myself, while very difficult, is the single most important thing I can do as a husband.

**Today was a great day because…**

1) my daughter responded to text messages today
2) traffic was light today
3) able to have lunch with Gary today

**I could have made today better by…**

taking sufficient time to calm down before reprimanding my son for his messy room

**Personal Notes**

Schedule meeting with Jim for tomorrow

# Let's Journal!

Date: ____/____/____

*However, let each one of you love his wife as himself, and let the wife see that she respects her husband.*

**Ephesians 5:33 (ESV)**

## I am thankful for…

1) ________________________________

2) ________________________________

3) ________________________________

## Scripture Reflection

________________________________

________________________________

________________________________

## Affirmation — I am…

________________________________

________________________________

________________________________

## Personal Notes

________________________________

________________________________

________________________________

________________________________

________________________________

________________________________

________________________________

________________________________

*"Whether we are husband or wife, we are not to live for ourselves but for the other. And that is the hardest yet single most important function of being a husband or a wife in marriage."*

**Timothy J. Keller**

## Quote Reflection

______________________________________________

______________________________________________

______________________________________________

## Today was a great day because…

1)____________________________________________

2)____________________________________________

3)____________________________________________

## I could have made today better by…

______________________________________________

______________________________________________

______________________________________________

## Personal Notes

______________________________________________

______________________________________________

______________________________________________

______________________________________________

______________________________________________

______________________________________________

______________________________________________

______________________________________________

Date: ____/____/____

*Train up a child in the way he should go;*
*even when he is old he will not depart from it.*
**Proverbs 22:6 (ESV)**

## I am thankful for…

1) ______________________________
2) ______________________________
3) ______________________________

## Scripture Reflection

______________________________
______________________________
______________________________

## Affirmation — I am…

______________________________
______________________________
______________________________

## Personal Notes

______________________________
______________________________
______________________________
______________________________
______________________________
______________________________
______________________________
______________________________

*"We're parents first, and once you have kids, everybody knows that you have priority lists. Number one is your family and everything else just kind of finds its place."*

**Tim McGraw**

## Quote Reflection

______________________________________________

______________________________________________

______________________________________________

## Today was a great day because...

1)____________________________________________

2)____________________________________________

3)____________________________________________

## I could have made today better by...

______________________________________________

______________________________________________

______________________________________________

## Personal Notes

______________________________________________

______________________________________________

______________________________________________

______________________________________________

______________________________________________

______________________________________________

______________________________________________

______________________________________________

Date: ____/____/________

*Beloved, let us love one another, for love is from God, and whoever loves has been born of God and knows God.*

**Ephesians 5:33 (ESV)**

**I am thankful for…**

1)______________________________

2)______________________________

3)______________________________

**Scripture Reflection**

______________________________

______________________________

______________________________

**Affirmation — I am…**

______________________________

______________________________

______________________________

**Personal Notes**

______________________________

______________________________

______________________________

______________________________

______________________________

______________________________

______________________________

______________________________

*"A good marriage requires time. It requires effort. You have to work at it. You have to cultivate it. You have to forgive and forget. You have to be absolutely loyal to one another."*

**Gordon B. Hinckley**

**Quote Reflection**

___

___

___

**Today was a great day because…**

1)___

2)___

3)___

**I could have made today better by…**

___

___

___

**Personal Notes**

___

___

___

___

___

___

___

___

Date: _____/_____/_____

*Grandchildren are the crown of the aged,*
*and the glory of children is their fathers.*
**Proverbs 17:6 (ESV)**

**I am thankful for…**

**1)**________________________________________

**2)**________________________________________

**3)**________________________________________

**Scripture Reflection**

**Affirmation — I am…**

**Personal Notes**

*"Let us sacrifice our today so that*
*our children can have a better tomorrow."*
**A.P.J. Abdul Kalam**

**Quote Reflection**

______________________________________________

______________________________________________

______________________________________________

**Today was a great day because…**

1)____________________________________________

2)____________________________________________

3)____________________________________________

**I could have made today better by…**

______________________________________________

______________________________________________

______________________________________________

**Personal Notes**

______________________________________________

______________________________________________

______________________________________________

______________________________________________

______________________________________________

______________________________________________

______________________________________________

______________________________________________

Date: ____/____/____

*But if anyone does not provide for his relatives,*
*and especially for members of his household,*
*he has denied the faith and is worse than an unbeliever.*
**1 Timothy 5:8 (ESV)**

**I am thankful for…**

1) ______________________________
2) ______________________________
3) ______________________________

**Scripture Reflection**

______________________________
______________________________
______________________________

**Affirmation — I am…**

______________________________
______________________________
______________________________

**Personal Notes**

______________________________
______________________________
______________________________
______________________________
______________________________
______________________________
______________________________
______________________________

*"Only when marriage and family exist for God's glory, and not to serve as replacement idols, are we able to truly love and be loved. Remember neither your child nor your husband (or wife) should be the one you worship, but instead who you worship with."*

**Mark Driscoll**

## Quote Reflection

______________________________

______________________________

______________________________

## Today was a great day because…

1)______________________________

2)______________________________

3)______________________________

## I could have made today better by…

______________________________

______________________________

______________________________

## Personal Notes

______________________________

______________________________

______________________________

______________________________

______________________________

______________________________

______________________________

______________________________

Date: ____/____/____

*In the same way husbands should love their wives as their own bodies. He who loves his wife loves himself.*
**Ephesians 5:28 (ESV)**

**I am thankful for…**

**1)**____________________

**2)**____________________

**3)**____________________

**Scripture Reflection**

____________________

____________________

____________________

**Affirmation — I am…**

____________________

____________________

____________________

**Personal Notes**

____________________

____________________

____________________

____________________

____________________

____________________

____________________

____________________

*"Many marriages would be better if the husband and wife clearly understood that they are on the same side."*

**Zig Ziglar**

## Quote Reflection

__________________________________________________

__________________________________________________

__________________________________________________

## Today was a great day because…

**1)**______________________________________________

**2)**______________________________________________

**3)**______________________________________________

## I could have made today better by…

__________________________________________________

__________________________________________________

__________________________________________________

## Personal Notes

__________________________________________________

__________________________________________________

__________________________________________________

__________________________________________________

__________________________________________________

__________________________________________________

__________________________________________________

__________________________________________________

Date: ____/____/____

*A wife of noble character who can find?*
*She is worth far more than rubies.*
**Proverbs 31:10 (NIV)**

**I am thankful for…**

1) ____________________

2) ____________________

3) ____________________

**Scripture Reflection**

____________________

____________________

____________________

**Affirmation — I am…**

____________________

____________________

____________________

**Personal Notes**

____________________

____________________

____________________

____________________

____________________

____________________

____________________

____________________

*"Happy marriages look to the future not the past."*

**Dale Partridge**

## Quote Reflection

______________________________________________

______________________________________________

______________________________________________

## Today was a great day because…

1)____________________________________________

2)____________________________________________

3)____________________________________________

## I could have made today better by…

______________________________________________

______________________________________________

______________________________________________

## Personal Notes

______________________________________________

______________________________________________

______________________________________________

______________________________________________

______________________________________________

______________________________________________

______________________________________________

______________________________________________

Date: ______/______/______

*Fathers, do not provoke your children to anger,*
*but bring them up in the discipline and instruction of the Lord.*
**Ephesians 6:4 (ESV)**

**I am thankful for…**

**1)**________________________________

**2)**________________________________

**3)**________________________________

**Scripture Reflection**

**Affirmation — I am…**

**Personal Notes**

*"It is not what you do for your children, but what you teach them to do for themselves, that will make them successful human beings."*
**Ann Landers**

**Quote Reflection**

______________________________

______________________________

______________________________

**Today was a great day because…**

1)______________________________

2)______________________________

3)______________________________

**I could have made today better by…**

______________________________

______________________________

______________________________

**Personal Notes**

______________________________

______________________________

______________________________

______________________________

______________________________

______________________________

______________________________

______________________________

Date: ____/____/____

*Gray hair is a crown of glory; it is gained in a righteous life.*

**Proverbs 16:31 (ESV)**

**I am thankful for…**

1) ______________________________

2) ______________________________

3) ______________________________

**Scripture Reflection**

______________________________

______________________________

______________________________

**Affirmation — I am…**

______________________________

______________________________

______________________________

**Personal Notes**

______________________________

______________________________

______________________________

______________________________

______________________________

______________________________

______________________________

______________________________

*"Young people need something stable to hang on to — a culture connection, a sense of their own past, a hope for their own future. Most of all, they need what grandparents can give them."*
**Jay Kesler**

## Quote Reflection

________________________________________

________________________________________

________________________________________

## Today was a great day because…

**1)**______________________________________

**2)**______________________________________

**3)**______________________________________

## I could have made today better by…

________________________________________

________________________________________

________________________________________

## Personal Notes

________________________________________

________________________________________

________________________________________

________________________________________

________________________________________

________________________________________

________________________________________

________________________________________

Date: ____/____/____

*Houses and wealth are inherited from parents,*
*but a prudent wife is from the LORD.*
**Proverbs 19:14 (NIV)**

**I am thankful for…**

1)

2)

3)

**Scripture Reflection**

**Affirmation — I am…**

**Personal Notes**

*"The best inheritance a parent can give his children is a few minutes of his time each day."*

**Orlando Aloysius Battista**

**Quote Reflection**

______________________________________________

______________________________________________

______________________________________________

**Today was a great day because…**

**1)**___________________________________________

**2)**___________________________________________

**3)**___________________________________________

**I could have made today better by…**

______________________________________________

______________________________________________

______________________________________________

**Personal Notes**

______________________________________________

______________________________________________

______________________________________________

______________________________________________

______________________________________________

______________________________________________

______________________________________________

______________________________________________

Date: ____/____/____

*A wife of noble character is her husband's crown,*
*but a disgraceful wife is like decay in his bones.*
**Proverbs 12:4 (NIV)**

**I am thankful for…**

**1)** ______________________________

**2)** ______________________________

**3)** ______________________________

**Scripture Reflection**

______________________________

______________________________

______________________________

**Affirmation — I am…**

______________________________

______________________________

______________________________

**Personal Notes**

______________________________

______________________________

______________________________

______________________________

______________________________

______________________________

______________________________

______________________________

*"To fully know and still fully love is the primary aim of marriage."*
**Ryan Frederick**

## Quote Reflection

______________________________________________

______________________________________________

______________________________________________

## Today was a great day because…

1)____________________________________________

2)____________________________________________

3)____________________________________________

## I could have made today better by…

______________________________________________

______________________________________________

______________________________________________

## Personal Notes

______________________________________________

______________________________________________

______________________________________________

______________________________________________

______________________________________________

______________________________________________

______________________________________________

______________________________________________

Date: ______ / ______ / ______

*Wives, submit yourselves to your husbands, as is fitting in the Lord. Husbands, love your wives and do not be harsh with them.*

**Colossians 3:18-19 (NIV)**

## I am thankful for…

1) ____________________

2) ____________________

3) ____________________

## Scripture Reflection

____________________

____________________

____________________

## Affirmation — I am…

____________________

____________________

____________________

## Personal Notes

____________________

____________________

____________________

____________________

____________________

____________________

____________________

____________________

*"A marriage cannot survive when we think only of ourselves. We need to recognize that to love someone is a choice, not a feeling."*
**Christin Slade**

## Quote Reflection

______________________________________________

______________________________________________

______________________________________________

## Today was a great day because…

1)____________________________________________

2)____________________________________________

3)____________________________________________

## I could have made today better by…

______________________________________________

______________________________________________

______________________________________________

## Personal Notes

______________________________________________

______________________________________________

______________________________________________

______________________________________________

______________________________________________

______________________________________________

______________________________________________

______________________________________________

Date: ____ / ____ / ____

*Behold, children are a heritage from the Lord, the fruit of the womb a reward. Like arrows in the hand of a warrior are the children of one's youth. Blessed is the man who fills his quiver with them! He shall not be put to shame when he speaks with his enemies in the gate.*

**Psalm 127:3-5 (ESV)**

**I am thankful for…**

1) ____________________

2) ____________________

3) ____________________

**Scripture Reflection**

____________________

____________________

____________________

**Affirmation — I am…**

____________________

____________________

____________________

**Personal Notes**

____________________

____________________

____________________

____________________

____________________

____________________

____________________

____________________

*"Children are not a distraction from more important work.*
*They are the most important work."*
**C.S. Lewis**

**Quote Reflection**

___
___
___

**Today was a great day because…**

1)___
2)___
3)___

**I could have made today better by…**

___
___
___

**Personal Notes**

___
___
___
___
___
___
___
___

Date: ____/____/____

*The rod and reproof give wisdom,*
*but a child left to himself brings shame to his mother.*
**Proverbs 29:15 (ESV)**

**I am thankful for…**

1)______________________________

2)______________________________

3)______________________________

**Scripture Reflection**

______________________________

______________________________

______________________________

**Affirmation — I am…**

______________________________

______________________________

______________________________

**Personal Notes**

______________________________

______________________________

______________________________

______________________________

______________________________

______________________________

______________________________

______________________________

*"I don't want my children to be what I want them to be.*
*I want them to become everything God created them to be."*
**Jon Gordon**

## Quote Reflection

______________________________________________

______________________________________________

______________________________________________

## Today was a great day because…

1)____________________________________________

2)____________________________________________

3)____________________________________________

## I could have made today better by…

______________________________________________

______________________________________________

______________________________________________

## Personal Notes

______________________________________________

______________________________________________

______________________________________________

______________________________________________

______________________________________________

______________________________________________

______________________________________________

______________________________________________

Date: ____/____/____

*And these words that I command you today shall be on your heart. You shall teach them diligently to your children, and shall talk of them when you sit in your house, and when you walk by the way, and when you lie down, and when you rise.*

**Deuteronomy 6:6-7 (ESV)**

**I am thankful for…**

**1)**________________________________

**2)**________________________________

**3)**________________________________

**Scripture Reflection**

________________________________

________________________________

________________________________

**Affirmation — I am…**

________________________________

________________________________

________________________________

**Personal Notes**

________________________________

________________________________

________________________________

________________________________

________________________________

________________________________

________________________________

________________________________

*"Children must be taught how to think, not what to think."*
**Margaret Mead**

## Quote Reflection

______________________________________________

______________________________________________

______________________________________________

## Today was a great day because…

1)____________________________________________

2)____________________________________________

3)____________________________________________

## I could have made today better by…

______________________________________________

______________________________________________

______________________________________________

## Personal Notes

______________________________________________

______________________________________________

______________________________________________

______________________________________________

______________________________________________

______________________________________________

______________________________________________

______________________________________________

Date: ____/____/____

*Let no one despise you for your youth, but set the believers an example in speech, in conduct, in love, in faith, in purity.*
**1 Timothy 4:12 (NIV)**

**I am thankful for…**

1) ______________________________

2) ______________________________

3) ______________________________

**Scripture Reflection**

______________________________

______________________________

______________________________

**Affirmation — I am…**

______________________________

______________________________

______________________________

**Personal Notes**

______________________________

______________________________

______________________________

______________________________

______________________________

______________________________

______________________________

______________________________

*"Good parents give their children roots and wings. Roots to know where home is, wings to fly away and exercise what's been taught them."*

**Jonas Salk**

## Quote Reflection

______________________________________________

______________________________________________

______________________________________________

## Today was a great day because…

1)____________________________________________

2)____________________________________________

3)____________________________________________

## I could have made today better by…

______________________________________________

______________________________________________

______________________________________________

## Personal Notes

______________________________________________

______________________________________________

______________________________________________

______________________________________________

______________________________________________

______________________________________________

______________________________________________

______________________________________________

Date: ____/____/____

*Above all, keep loving one another earnestly, since love covers a multitude of sins.*
**1 Peter 4:8 (ESV)**

**I am thankful for…**

1) ____________________
2) ____________________
3) ____________________

**Scripture Reflection**

____________________
____________________
____________________

**Affirmation — I am…**

____________________
____________________
____________________

**Personal Notes**

____________________
____________________
____________________
____________________
____________________
____________________
____________________
____________________

*"I sustain myself with the love of family."*
**Maya Angelou**

## Quote Reflection

______________________________

______________________________

______________________________

## Today was a great day because…

1)______________________________

2)______________________________

3)______________________________

## I could have made today better by…

______________________________

______________________________

______________________________

## Personal Notes

______________________________

______________________________

______________________________

______________________________

______________________________

______________________________

______________________________

______________________________

Date: ____/____/____

*Her children rise up and call her blessed;*
*her husband also, and he praises her:*
**Proverbs 31:28 (ESV)**

**I am thankful for…**

1)____________________

2)____________________

3)____________________

**Scripture Reflection**

____________________

____________________

____________________

**Affirmation — I am…**

____________________

____________________

____________________

**Personal Notes**

____________________

____________________

____________________

____________________

____________________

____________________

____________________

____________________

*"Marriages are like fingerprints;*
*each one is different and each one is beautiful."*
**Maggie Reyes**

## Quote Reflection

______________________________________________

______________________________________________

______________________________________________

## Today was a great day because...

1)______________________________________________

2)______________________________________________

3)______________________________________________

## I could have made today better by...

______________________________________________

______________________________________________

______________________________________________

## Personal Notes

______________________________________________

______________________________________________

______________________________________________

______________________________________________

______________________________________________

______________________________________________

______________________________________________

______________________________________________

Date: ____/____/______

*Husbands, love your wives, as Christ loved the church and gave himself up for her*
**Ephesians 5:25 (ESV)**

**I am thankful for…**

1)______________________________

2)______________________________

3)______________________________

**Scripture Reflection**

______________________________

______________________________

______________________________

**Affirmation — I am…**

______________________________

______________________________

______________________________

**Personal Notes**

______________________________

______________________________

______________________________

______________________________

______________________________

______________________________

______________________________

______________________________

*"The best time to love with your whole heart is always now, in this moment, because no breath beyond the current is promised."*
**Fawn Weaver**

**Quote Reflection**

______________________________

______________________________

______________________________

**Today was a great day because…**

1)______________________________

2)______________________________

3)______________________________

**I could have made today better by…**

______________________________

______________________________

______________________________

**Personal Notes**

______________________________

______________________________

______________________________

______________________________

______________________________

______________________________

______________________________

______________________________

Date: ____/____/____

*Charm is deceitful, and beauty is vain,*
*but a woman who fears the Lord is to be praised.*
**Proverbs 31:30 (ESV)**

**I am thankful for…**

1) ____________________
2) ____________________
3) ____________________

**Scripture Reflection**

____________________
____________________
____________________

**Affirmation — I am…**

____________________
____________________
____________________

**Personal Notes**

____________________
____________________
____________________
____________________
____________________
____________________
____________________
____________________

*"Success in marriage does not come merely through finding the right mate, but through being the right mate."*
**Barnett R. Brickner**

**Quote Reflection**

______________________________________________

______________________________________________

______________________________________________

**Today was a great day because…**

**1)**____________________________________________

**2)**____________________________________________

**3)**____________________________________________

**I could have made today better by…**

______________________________________________

______________________________________________

______________________________________________

**Personal Notes**

______________________________________________

______________________________________________

______________________________________________

______________________________________________

______________________________________________

______________________________________________

______________________________________________

______________________________________________

Date: ____/____/____

*He and all his family were devout and God-fearing;*
*he gave generously to those in need and prayed to God regularly.*
**Acts 10:2 (NIV)**

**I am thankful for…**

**1)**________________________________________

**2)**________________________________________

**3)**________________________________________

**Scripture Reflection**

________________________________________

________________________________________

________________________________________

**Affirmation — I am…**

________________________________________

________________________________________

________________________________________

**Personal Notes**

________________________________________

________________________________________

________________________________________

________________________________________

________________________________________

________________________________________

________________________________________

________________________________________

*"A happy family is but an earlier heaven."*
**George Bernard Shaw**

## Quote Reflection

______________________________________________

______________________________________________

______________________________________________

## Today was a great day because…

1)____________________________________________

2)____________________________________________

3)____________________________________________

## I could have made today better by…

______________________________________________

______________________________________________

______________________________________________

## Personal Notes

______________________________________________

______________________________________________

______________________________________________

______________________________________________

______________________________________________

______________________________________________

______________________________________________

______________________________________________

Date: ____/____/____

*To the married I give this charge (not I, but the Lord): the wife should not separate from her husband*

**1 Corinthians 7:10 (ESV)**

## I am thankful for…

1)______________________________

2)______________________________

3)______________________________

## Scripture Reflection

## Affirmation — I am…

## Personal Notes

*"Love one another and you will be happy.*
*It's as simple and as difficult as that."*
**Michael Leunig**

## Quote Reflection

______________________________________________

______________________________________________

______________________________________________

## Today was a great day because…

1)____________________________________________

2)____________________________________________

3)____________________________________________

## I could have made today better by…

______________________________________________

______________________________________________

______________________________________________

## Personal Notes

______________________________________________

______________________________________________

______________________________________________

______________________________________________

______________________________________________

______________________________________________

______________________________________________

______________________________________________

Date: ____/____/________

*He who finds a wife finds what is good and receives favor from the LORD.*
**Proverbs 8:22 (NIV)**

**I am thankful for…**

1)________________________________________

2)________________________________________

3)________________________________________

**Scripture Reflection**

________________________________________

________________________________________

________________________________________

**Affirmation — I am…**

________________________________________

________________________________________

________________________________________

**Personal Notes**

________________________________________

________________________________________

________________________________________

________________________________________

________________________________________

________________________________________

________________________________________

________________________________________

*"The goal in marriage is not to think alike, but to think together."*

**Robert C. Dodds**

## Quote Reflection

______________________________________________

______________________________________________

______________________________________________

## Today was a great day because…

1)____________________________________________

2)____________________________________________

3)____________________________________________

## I could have made today better by…

______________________________________________

______________________________________________

______________________________________________

## Personal Notes

______________________________________________

______________________________________________

______________________________________________

______________________________________________

______________________________________________

______________________________________________

______________________________________________

______________________________________________

Date: ____/____/________

*Many claim to have unfailing love, but a faithful person who can find? The righteous lead blameless lives; blessed are their children after them.*

**Proverbs 20:6-7 (NIV)**

## I am thankful for…

1) ______________________________

2) ______________________________

3) ______________________________

## Scripture Reflection

______________________________

______________________________

______________________________

## Affirmation — I am…

______________________________

______________________________

______________________________

## Personal Notes

______________________________

______________________________

______________________________

______________________________

______________________________

______________________________

______________________________

______________________________

*"I think togetherness is a very important ingredient to family life."*
**Barbara Bush**

## Quote Reflection

______________________________________________

______________________________________________

______________________________________________

## Today was a great day because…

1)____________________________________________

2)____________________________________________

3)____________________________________________

## I could have made today better by…

______________________________________________

______________________________________________

______________________________________________

## Personal Notes

______________________________________________

______________________________________________

______________________________________________

______________________________________________

______________________________________________

______________________________________________

______________________________________________

______________________________________________

Date: ____/____/____

*If a man has recently married, he must not be sent to war or have any other duty laid on him. For one year he is to be free to stay at home and bring happiness to the wife he has married.*

**Deuteronomy 24:5 (NIV)**

**I am thankful for…**

**1)**______________________________

**2)**______________________________

**3)**______________________________

**Scripture Reflection**

______________________________

______________________________

______________________________

**Affirmation — I am…**

______________________________

______________________________

______________________________

**Personal Notes**

______________________________

______________________________

______________________________

______________________________

______________________________

______________________________

______________________________

______________________________

*"Marriage is an act of will that signifies and involves a mutual gift, which unites the spouses and binds them to their eventual souls, with whom they make up a sole family – a domestic church."*
**Pope John Paul II**

**Quote Reflection**

______________________________________________

______________________________________________

______________________________________________

**Today was a great day because…**

1)____________________________________________

2)____________________________________________

3)____________________________________________

**I could have made today better by…**

______________________________________________

______________________________________________

______________________________________________

**Personal Notes**

______________________________________________

______________________________________________

______________________________________________

______________________________________________

______________________________________________

______________________________________________

______________________________________________

______________________________________________

Date: ____/____/____

*Then the LORD God made a woman from the rib he had taken out of the man, and he brought her to the man. The man said, "This is now bone of my bones and flesh of my flesh; she shall be called 'woman,' for she was taken out of man." That is why a man leaves his father and mother and is united to his wife, and they become one flesh.*

**Genesis 2:22-24 (NIV)**

**I am thankful for…**

**1)**______________________________

**2)**______________________________

**3)**______________________________

**Scripture Reflection**

______________________________

______________________________

______________________________

**Affirmation — I am…**

______________________________

______________________________

______________________________

**Personal Notes**

______________________________

______________________________

______________________________

______________________________

______________________________

______________________________

______________________________

______________________________

*"A happy marriage is about three things: memories of togetherness, forgiveness of mistakes and a promise to never give up on each other."*
**Surabhi Surendra**

## Quote Reflection

________________________________________

________________________________________

________________________________________

## Today was a great day because…

1)____________________________________

2)____________________________________

3)____________________________________

## I could have made today better by…

________________________________________

________________________________________

________________________________________

## Personal Notes

________________________________________

________________________________________

________________________________________

________________________________________

________________________________________

________________________________________

________________________________________

________________________________________

Date: ____/____/____

*For as a young man marries a young woman, so shall your sons marry you, and as the bridegroom rejoices over the bride, so shall your God rejoice over you.*

**Isaiah 62:5 (ESV)**

## I am thankful for…

1) ______________________________
2) ______________________________
3) ______________________________

## Scripture Reflection

______________________________
______________________________
______________________________

## Affirmation — I am…

______________________________
______________________________
______________________________

## Personal Notes

______________________________
______________________________
______________________________
______________________________
______________________________
______________________________
______________________________
______________________________

*"The real act of marriage takes place in the heart, not in the ballroom or church or synagogue. It's a choice you make — not just on your wedding day, but over and over again — and that choice is reflected in the way you treat your husband or wife."*

**Barbara De Angelis**

## Quote Reflection

________________________________________

________________________________________

________________________________________

## Today was a great day because…

1)______________________________________

2)______________________________________

3)______________________________________

## I could have made today better by…

________________________________________

________________________________________

________________________________________

## Personal Notes

________________________________________

________________________________________

________________________________________

________________________________________

________________________________________

________________________________________

________________________________________

________________________________________

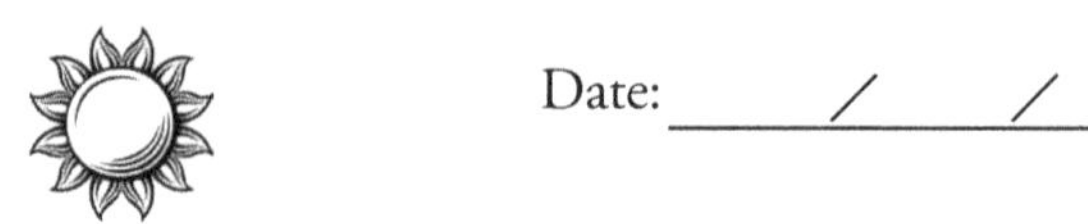

Date: ______ / ______ / ______

*Then children were brought to him that he might lay his hands on them and pray. The disciples rebuked the people, but Jesus said, "Let the little children come to me and do not hinder them, for to such belongs the kingdom of heaven."*

**Matthew 19:13-14 (ESV)**

**I am thankful for…**

**1)**______________________________

**2)**______________________________

**3)**______________________________

**Scripture Reflection**

______________________________

______________________________

______________________________

**Affirmation — I am…**

______________________________

______________________________

______________________________

**Personal Notes**

______________________________

______________________________

______________________________

______________________________

______________________________

______________________________

______________________________

______________________________

*"There is no job more important than parenting. This I believe."*
**Ben Carson**

## Quote Reflection

______________________________________________

______________________________________________

______________________________________________

## Today was a great day because…

1)____________________________________________

2)____________________________________________

3)____________________________________________

## I could have made today better by…

______________________________________________

______________________________________________

______________________________________________

## Personal Notes

______________________________________________

______________________________________________

______________________________________________

______________________________________________

______________________________________________

______________________________________________

______________________________________________

______________________________________________

Date: ____/____/____

*Do not withhold discipline from a child; if you strike him with a rod, he will not die. If you strike him with the rod, you will save his soul from Sheol.*

**Proverbs 23:13-14 (ESV)**

**I am thankful for…**

1)________________________________________

2)________________________________________

3)________________________________________

**Scripture Reflection**

________________________________________

________________________________________

________________________________________

**Affirmation — I am…**

________________________________________

________________________________________

________________________________________

**Personal Notes**

________________________________________

________________________________________

________________________________________

________________________________________

________________________________________

________________________________________

________________________________________

________________________________________

*"The family teaches us about the importance of knowledge, education, hard work, and effort. It teaches us about enjoying ourselves, having fun, keeping fit and healthy."*
**Kamisese Mara**

**Quote Reflection**

______________________________________________

______________________________________________

______________________________________________

**Today was a great day because…**

**1)**____________________________________________

**2)**____________________________________________

**3)**____________________________________________

**I could have made today better by…**

______________________________________________

______________________________________________

______________________________________________

**Personal Notes**

______________________________________________

______________________________________________

______________________________________________

______________________________________________

______________________________________________

______________________________________________

______________________________________________

______________________________________________

Date: ____/____/____

*Likewise, you who are younger, be subject to the elders. Clothe yourselves, all of you, with humility toward one another, for "God opposes the proud but gives grace to the humble."*

**1 Peter 5:5 (ESV)**

**I am thankful for…**

**1)**____________________

**2)**____________________

**3)**____________________

**Scripture Reflection**

**Affirmation — I am…**

**Personal Notes**

*"Nothing you do for your children is ever wasted. They seem not to notice us, hovering, averting our eyes, and they seldom offer thanks, but what we do for them is never wasted."*

**Garrison Keillor**

**Quote Reflection**

______________________________________________

______________________________________________

______________________________________________

**Today was a great day because…**

1)____________________________________________

2)____________________________________________

3)____________________________________________

**I could have made today better by…**

______________________________________________

______________________________________________

______________________________________________

**Personal Notes**

______________________________________________

______________________________________________

______________________________________________

______________________________________________

______________________________________________

______________________________________________

______________________________________________

______________________________________________

Date: ____/____/____

*The proverbs of Solomon. A wise son makes a glad father, but a foolish son is a sorrow to his mother.*
**Proverbs 10:1 (ESV)**

**I am thankful for…**

1)____________________

2)____________________

3)____________________

**Scripture Reflection**

____________________

____________________

____________________

**Affirmation — I am…**

____________________

____________________

____________________

**Personal Notes**

____________________

____________________

____________________

____________________

____________________

____________________

____________________

____________________

*"Success for me is to raise happy, healthy human beings."*

**Kelly LeBrock**

## Quote Reflection

______________________________________________

______________________________________________

______________________________________________

## Today was a great day because…

1)____________________________________________

2)____________________________________________

3)____________________________________________

## I could have made today better by…

______________________________________________

______________________________________________

______________________________________________

## Personal Notes

______________________________________________

______________________________________________

______________________________________________

______________________________________________

______________________________________________

______________________________________________

______________________________________________

______________________________________________

Date: ____/____/____

*Discipline your son, for there is hope;*
*do not set your heart on putting him to death.*
**Proverbs 19:18 (ESV))**

**I am thankful for…**

**1)**______________________________

**2)**______________________________

**3)**______________________________

**Scripture Reflection**

______________________________

______________________________

______________________________

**Affirmation — I am…**

______________________________

______________________________

______________________________

**Personal Notes**

______________________________

______________________________

______________________________

______________________________

______________________________

______________________________

______________________________

______________________________

*"The gain is not the having of children;*
*it is the discovery of love and how to be loving."*
**Polly Berrein Berends**

## Quote Reflection

______________________________

______________________________

______________________________

## Today was a great day because…

1)______________________________

2)______________________________

3)______________________________

## I could have made today better by…

______________________________

______________________________

______________________________

## Personal Notes

______________________________

______________________________

______________________________

______________________________

______________________________

______________________________

______________________________

______________________________

Date: ____/____/____

*However, let each one of you love his wife as himself, and let the wife see that she respects her husband.*
**Ephesians 5:33 (ESV)**

**I am thankful for…**

1)____________________

2)____________________

3)____________________

**Scripture Reflection**

**Affirmation — I am…**

**Personal Notes**

*"Whether we are husband or wife, we are not to live for ourselves but for the other. And that is the hardest yet single most important function of being a husband or a wife in marriage."*

**Timothy J. Keller**

## Quote Reflection

____________________________________________

____________________________________________

____________________________________________

## Today was a great day because…

**1)**__________________________________________

**2)**__________________________________________

**3)**__________________________________________

## I could have made today better by…

____________________________________________

____________________________________________

____________________________________________

## Personal Notes

____________________________________________

____________________________________________

____________________________________________

____________________________________________

____________________________________________

____________________________________________

____________________________________________

____________________________________________

Date: ____/____/____

*Little children, keep yourselves from idols.*

**1 John 5:21 (ESV)**

**I am thankful for…**

1)______________________________

2)______________________________

3)______________________________

**Scripture Reflection**

______________________________

______________________________

______________________________

**Affirmation — I am…**

______________________________

______________________________

______________________________

**Personal Notes**

______________________________

______________________________

______________________________

______________________________

______________________________

______________________________

______________________________

______________________________

*"I came to parenting the way most of us do — knowing nothing and trying to learn everything."*
**Mayim Bialik**

## Quote Reflection

______________________________________________

______________________________________________

______________________________________________

## Today was a great day because…

1)____________________________________________

2)____________________________________________

3)____________________________________________

## I could have made today better by…

______________________________________________

______________________________________________

______________________________________________

## Personal Notes

______________________________________________

______________________________________________

______________________________________________

______________________________________________

______________________________________________

______________________________________________

______________________________________________

______________________________________________

Date: ____/____/____

*Your wife will be like a fruitful vine within your house;*
*your children will be like olive shoots around your table.*
**Psalm 128:3 (ESV)**

**I am thankful for…**

1)______________________________
2)______________________________
3)______________________________

**Scripture Reflection**

______________________________
______________________________
______________________________

**Affirmation — I am…**

______________________________
______________________________
______________________________

**Personal Notes**

______________________________
______________________________
______________________________
______________________________
______________________________
______________________________
______________________________
______________________________

*"We go into parenting, and we discover that we don't have the answers. We are at a loss."*

**Julia Cameron**

## Quote Reflection

________________________________________

________________________________________

________________________________________

## Today was a great day because…

1)______________________________________

2)______________________________________

3)______________________________________

## I could have made today better by…

________________________________________

________________________________________

________________________________________

## Personal Notes

________________________________________

________________________________________

________________________________________

________________________________________

________________________________________

________________________________________

________________________________________

________________________________________

Date: ____/____/____

*Even to your old age I am he, and to gray hairs I will carry you. I have made, and I will bear; I will carry and will save.*
**Isaiah 46:4 (ESV)**

**I am thankful for…**

1)____________________

2)____________________

3)____________________

**Scripture Reflection**

____________________

____________________

____________________

**Affirmation — I am…**

____________________

____________________

____________________

**Personal Notes**

____________________

____________________

____________________

____________________

____________________

____________________

____________________

____________________

*"The children who are 'our future' will inherit a world created not just by parental devotion but by the sort of zealous, focused endeavors that can preclude good parenting."*
**Virginia Postrel**

## Quote Reflection

______________________________________________

______________________________________________

______________________________________________

## Today was a great day because…

1)____________________________________________

2)____________________________________________

3)____________________________________________

## I could have made today better by…

______________________________________________

______________________________________________

______________________________________________

## Personal Notes

______________________________________________

______________________________________________

______________________________________________

______________________________________________

______________________________________________

______________________________________________

______________________________________________

______________________________________________

Date: ___/___/___

*For if someone does not know how to manage his own household, how will he care for God's church?*
**1 Timothy 3:5 (ESV)**

**I am thankful for…**

1)______________________________
2)______________________________
3)______________________________

**Scripture Reflection**

______________________________
______________________________
______________________________

**Affirmation — I am…**

______________________________
______________________________
______________________________

**Personal Notes**

______________________________
______________________________
______________________________
______________________________
______________________________
______________________________
______________________________
______________________________

*"I learned that life is about the people around you and the people you give back to. That's what parenting is: You're not there for yourself; you're there for your offspring and everyone else around you."*

**Conrad Anker**

## Quote Reflection

________________________________________

________________________________________

________________________________________

## Today was a great day because…

1)______________________________________

2)______________________________________

3)______________________________________

## I could have made today better by…

________________________________________

________________________________________

________________________________________

## Personal Notes

________________________________________

________________________________________

________________________________________

________________________________________

________________________________________

________________________________________

________________________________________

________________________________________

Date: ____/____/____

*For if someone does not know how to manage his own household, how will he care for God's church?*

**1 Timothy 3:5 (ESV)**

**I am thankful for…**

1)________________________________

2)________________________________

3)________________________________

**Scripture Reflection**

________________________________

________________________________

________________________________

**Affirmation — I am…**

________________________________

________________________________

________________________________

**Personal Notes**

________________________________

________________________________

________________________________

________________________________

________________________________

________________________________

________________________________

________________________________

*"You can learn many things from your children. How much patience you have, for instance."*
**Franklin P. Jones**

## Quote Reflection

______________________________

______________________________

______________________________

## Today was a great day because…

1)______________________________

2)______________________________

3)______________________________

## I could have made today better by…

______________________________

______________________________

______________________________

## Personal Notes

______________________________

______________________________

______________________________

______________________________

______________________________

______________________________

______________________________

______________________________

Date: ____/____/____

*To the woman he said, "I will surely multiply your pain in childbearing; in pain you shall bring forth children. Your desire shall be for your husband, and he shall rule over you."*

**Genesis 3:16 (ESV)**

**I am thankful for…**

1) ____________________

2) ____________________

3) ____________________

**Scripture Reflection**

____________________

____________________

____________________

**Affirmation — I am…**

____________________

____________________

____________________

**Personal Notes**

____________________

____________________

____________________

____________________

____________________

____________________

____________________

____________________

*"Children should have enough freedom to be themselves — once they've learned the rules."*
**Anna Quindlen**

## Quote Reflection

________________________________________

________________________________________

________________________________________

## Today was a great day because…

**1)**______________________________________

**2)**______________________________________

**3)**______________________________________

## I could have made today better by…

________________________________________

________________________________________

________________________________________

## Personal Notes

________________________________________

________________________________________

________________________________________

________________________________________

________________________________________

________________________________________

________________________________________

________________________________________

Date: ____/____/____

*Likewise, wives, be subject to your own husbands,*
*so that even if some do not obey the word,*
*they may be won without a word by the conduct of their wives,*
**1 Peter 3:1 (ESV)**

**I am thankful for…**

1)______________________________

2)______________________________

3)______________________________

**Scripture Reflection**

______________________________

______________________________

______________________________

**Affirmation — I am…**

______________________________

______________________________

______________________________

**Personal Notes**

______________________________

______________________________

______________________________

______________________________

______________________________

______________________________

______________________________

______________________________

*"I suppose it's amazing how quick life goes by when you have children."*

**Steffi Graf**

## Quote Reflection

______________________________________________

______________________________________________

______________________________________________

## Today was a great day because…

1)____________________________________________

2)____________________________________________

3)____________________________________________

## I could have made today better by…

______________________________________________

______________________________________________

______________________________________________

## Personal Notes

______________________________________________

______________________________________________

______________________________________________

______________________________________________

______________________________________________

______________________________________________

______________________________________________

______________________________________________

Date: ____/____/____

*Then the Lord God said, "It is not good that the man should be alone; I will make him a helper fit for him."*
**Genesis 2:18 (ESV)**

**I am thankful for…**

1)______________________________
2)______________________________
3)______________________________

**Scripture Reflection**

______________________________
______________________________
______________________________

**Affirmation — I am…**

______________________________
______________________________
______________________________

**Personal Notes**

______________________________
______________________________
______________________________
______________________________
______________________________
______________________________
______________________________
______________________________

*"Nobody ever becomes an expert parent. But I think good parenting is about consistency. It's about being there at big moments, but its also just the consistency of decision making. And it's routine."*

**Sebastian Coe**

## Quote Reflection

________________________________________

________________________________________

________________________________________

## Today was a great day because…

**1)**______________________________________

**2)**______________________________________

**3)**______________________________________

## I could have made today better by…

________________________________________

________________________________________

________________________________________

## Personal Notes

________________________________________

________________________________________

________________________________________

________________________________________

________________________________________

________________________________________

________________________________________

________________________________________

Date: ____/____/____

*You shall stand up before the gray head and honor the face of an old man, and you shall fear your God: I am the Lord.*

**Leviticus 19:32 (ESV)**

**I am thankful for…**

1)______________________________

2)______________________________

3)______________________________

**Scripture Reflection**

**Affirmation — I am…**

**Personal Notes**

*"There is no such thing as a perfect parent. So just be a real one."*

**Sue Atkins**

## Quote Reflection

______________________________________________

______________________________________________

______________________________________________

## Today was a great day because…

1)____________________________________________

2)____________________________________________

3)____________________________________________

## I could have made today better by…

______________________________________________

______________________________________________

______________________________________________

## Personal Notes

______________________________________________

______________________________________________

______________________________________________

______________________________________________

______________________________________________

______________________________________________

______________________________________________

______________________________________________

Date: ____/____/________

*And he said to them, "You have a fine way of rejecting the commandment of God in order to establish your tradition! For Moses said, 'Honor your father and your mother'; and, 'Whoever reviles father or mother must surely die.' But you say, 'If a man tells his father or his mother, "Whatever you would have gained from me is Corban"' (that is, given to God)— then you no longer permit him to do anything for his father or mother, thus making void the word of God by your tradition that you have handed down. And many such things you do."*

**Mark 7:9-13 (ESV)**

## I am thankful for…

**1)**______________________________

**2)**______________________________

**3)**______________________________

## Scripture Reflection

______________________________

______________________________

______________________________

## Affirmation — I am…

______________________________

______________________________

______________________________

## Personal Notes

______________________________

______________________________

______________________________

______________________________

______________________________

______________________________

______________________________

______________________________

*"To be in your children's memories tomorrow, you have to be in their lives today."*

**Unknown**

## Quote Reflection

______________________________________________

______________________________________________

______________________________________________

## Today was a great day because…

1)____________________________________________

2)____________________________________________

3)____________________________________________

## I could have made today better by…

______________________________________________

______________________________________________

______________________________________________

## Personal Notes

______________________________________________

______________________________________________

______________________________________________

______________________________________________

______________________________________________

______________________________________________

______________________________________________

______________________________________________

Date: ____/____/____

*Older women as mothers, younger women as sisters, in all purity.*

**1 Timothy 5:2 (NIV)**

## I am thankful for…

1) ______________________________

2) ______________________________

3) ______________________________

## Scripture Reflection

______________________________

______________________________

______________________________

## Affirmation — I am…

______________________________

______________________________

______________________________

## Personal Notes

______________________________

______________________________

______________________________

______________________________

______________________________

______________________________

______________________________

______________________________

*"The sign of good parenting is not the child's behavior.*
*The sign of truly good parenting is the parent's behavior."*
**Andy Smithson**

## Quote Reflection

______________________________

______________________________

______________________________

## Today was a great day because…

1)______________________________

2)______________________________

3)______________________________

## I could have made today better by…

______________________________

______________________________

______________________________

## Personal Notes

______________________________

______________________________

______________________________

______________________________

______________________________

______________________________

______________________________

______________________________

Date: ____/____/____

*Then Esau looked up and saw the women and children. "Who are these with you?" he asked. Jacob answered, "They are the children God has graciously given your servant."*

**Genesis 33:5 (NIV)**

**I am thankful for…**

1)________________

2)________________

3)________________

**Scripture Reflection**

________________

________________

________________

**Affirmation — I am…**

________________

________________

________________

**Personal Notes**

________________

________________

________________

________________

________________

________________

________________

________________

*"Remember, the kids that need the most love will ask for it in the most unloving ways."*
**Russel Barkley**

## Quote Reflection

________________________________________
________________________________________
________________________________________

## Today was a great day because…

**1)**______________________________________
**2)**______________________________________
**3)**______________________________________

## I could have made today better by…

________________________________________
________________________________________
________________________________________

## Personal Notes

________________________________________
________________________________________
________________________________________
________________________________________
________________________________________
________________________________________
________________________________________
________________________________________

Date: ____/____/____

*He settles the childless woman in her home*
*as a happy mother of children. Praise the LORD.*
**Psalms 113:9 (NIV)**

**I am thankful for…**

1)____________________

2)____________________

3)____________________

**Scripture Reflection**

____________________

____________________

____________________

**Affirmation — I am…**

____________________

____________________

____________________

**Personal Notes**

____________________

____________________

____________________

____________________

____________________

____________________

____________________

____________________

*"Your children need your presence more than your presents."*
**Jesse Jackson**

## Quote Reflection

______________________________________________

______________________________________________

______________________________________________

## Today was a great day because…

1)____________________________________________

2)____________________________________________

3)____________________________________________

## I could have made today better by…

______________________________________________

______________________________________________

______________________________________________

## Personal Notes

______________________________________________

______________________________________________

______________________________________________

______________________________________________

______________________________________________

______________________________________________

______________________________________________

______________________________________________

Date: ____/____/____

*But as for you, continue in what you have learned and have become convinced of, because you know those from whom you learned it, and how from infancy you have known the Holy Scriptures, which are able to make you wise for salvation through faith in Christ Jesus.*

**2 Timothy 3:14-15 (NIV)**

**I am thankful for…**

**1)**______________________________

**2)**______________________________

**3)**______________________________

**Scripture Reflection**

______________________________

______________________________

______________________________

**Affirmation — I am…**

______________________________

______________________________

______________________________

**Personal Notes**

______________________________

______________________________

______________________________

______________________________

______________________________

______________________________

______________________________

______________________________

*"Kids are like a mirror, what they see and hear they do.*
*Be a good reflection for them."*
**K. Heath**

**Quote Reflection**

______________________________________________

______________________________________________

______________________________________________

**Today was a great day because…**

1)____________________________________________

2)____________________________________________

3)____________________________________________

**I could have made today better by…**

______________________________________________

______________________________________________

______________________________________________

**Personal Notes**

______________________________________________

______________________________________________

______________________________________________

______________________________________________

______________________________________________

______________________________________________

______________________________________________

______________________________________________

Date: ____/____/____

*See that you do not despise one of these little ones. For I tell you that their angels in heaven always see the face of my Father in heaven.*
**Matthew 18:10 (NIV)**

**I am thankful for…**

1)____________________

2)____________________

3)____________________

**Scripture Reflection**

____________________

____________________

____________________

**Affirmation — I am…**

____________________

____________________

____________________

**Personal Notes**

____________________

____________________

____________________

____________________

____________________

____________________

____________________

____________________

*"Parents are teachers, guides, leaders, protectors and providers for their children."*
**Iyanla Vanzant**

## Quote Reflection

______________________________________________

______________________________________________

______________________________________________

## Today was a great day because…

1)____________________________________________

2)____________________________________________

3)____________________________________________

## I could have made today better by…

______________________________________________

______________________________________________

______________________________________________

## Personal Notes

______________________________________________

______________________________________________

______________________________________________

______________________________________________

______________________________________________

______________________________________________

______________________________________________

______________________________________________

Date: ____/____/____

*Impress them on your children. Talk about them*
*when you sit at home and when you walk along the road,*
*when you lie down and when you get up.*
**Deuteronomy 6:7 (NIV)**

**I am thankful for…**

1)____________________

2)____________________

3)____________________

**Scripture Reflection**

____________________

____________________

____________________

**Affirmation — I am…**

____________________

____________________

____________________

**Personal Notes**

____________________

____________________

____________________

____________________

____________________

____________________

____________________

____________________

*"In marriage do thou be wise: prefer the person before money, virtue before beauty, then mind before the body; then thou hast a wife, a friend, a companion, a second self."*
**William Penn**

## Quote Reflection

___

___

___

## Today was a great day because…

1)___

2)___

3)___

## I could have made today better by…

___

___

___

## Personal Notes

___

___

___

___

___

___

___

___

Date: ____/____/____

*Listen, my son, to your father's instruction and do not forsake your mother's teaching. They are a garland to grace your head and a chain to adorn your neck.*

**Proverbs 1:8-9 (NIV)**

**I am thankful for…**

**1)**______________________________

**2)**______________________________

**3)**______________________________

**Scripture Reflection**

______________________________

______________________________

______________________________

**Affirmation — I am…**

______________________________

______________________________

______________________________

**Personal Notes**

______________________________

______________________________

______________________________

______________________________

______________________________

______________________________

______________________________

______________________________

*"Marriages, like careers, need constant nurturing... the secret of having it all is loving it all."*
**Joyce Brothers**

## Quote Reflection

______________________________________________

______________________________________________

______________________________________________

## Today was a great day because…

1)____________________________________________

2)____________________________________________

3)____________________________________________

## I could have made today better by…

______________________________________________

______________________________________________

______________________________________________

## Personal Notes

______________________________________________

______________________________________________

______________________________________________

______________________________________________

______________________________________________

______________________________________________

______________________________________________

______________________________________________

Date: ____/____/____

*Children, obey your parents in everything, for this pleases the Lord.*

**Colossians 3:20 (NIV)**

## I am thankful for…

1) ______________________

2) ______________________

3) ______________________

## Scripture Reflection

______________________

______________________

______________________

## Affirmation — I am…

______________________

______________________

______________________

## Personal Notes

______________________

______________________

______________________

______________________

______________________

______________________

______________________

______________________

*"Marriage is not a noun, it's a verb. It isn't something you get. It's something you do. It's the way you love your partner everyday."*

**Barbara De Angelis**

## Quote Reflection

______________________________________________

______________________________________________

______________________________________________

## Today was a great day because…

1)____________________________________________

2)____________________________________________

3)____________________________________________

## I could have made today better by…

______________________________________________

______________________________________________

______________________________________________

## Personal Notes

______________________________________________

______________________________________________

______________________________________________

______________________________________________

______________________________________________

______________________________________________

______________________________________________

______________________________________________

Date: ____/____/____

*Show yourself in all respects to be a model of good works, and in your teaching show integrity, dignity...*
**Titus 2:7 (ESV)**

**I am thankful for...**

1) ____________________
2) ____________________
3) ____________________

**Scripture Reflection**

____________________
____________________
____________________

**Affirmation — I am...**

____________________
____________________
____________________

**Personal Notes**

____________________
____________________
____________________
____________________
____________________
____________________
____________________
____________________

*"Happier is the wife who learns to hold on to Jesus tighter than she holds on to her husband."*

**Ngina Otiende**

## Quote Reflection

______________________________

______________________________

______________________________

## Today was a great day because…

1)______________________________

2)______________________________

3)______________________________

## I could have made today better by…

______________________________

______________________________

______________________________

## Personal Notes

______________________________

______________________________

______________________________

______________________________

______________________________

______________________________

______________________________

______________________________

Date: ____/____/____

*Discipline your son, and he will give you rest;*
*he will give delight to your heart.*
**Proverbs 29:17 (ESV)**

**I am thankful for…**

**1)**______________________________

**2)**______________________________

**3)**______________________________

**Scripture Reflection**

______________________________

______________________________

______________________________

**Affirmation — I am…**

______________________________

______________________________

______________________________

**Personal Notes**

______________________________

______________________________

______________________________

______________________________

______________________________

______________________________

______________________________

______________________________

*"There is no challenge strong enough to destroy your marriage as long as you are both willing to stop fighting against each other and start fighting for each other."*

**Dave Willis**

## Quote Reflection

________________________________________

________________________________________

________________________________________

## Today was a great day because...

1)______________________________________

2)______________________________________

3)______________________________________

## I could have made today better by...

________________________________________

________________________________________

________________________________________

## Personal Notes

________________________________________

________________________________________

________________________________________

________________________________________

________________________________________

________________________________________

________________________________________

________________________________________

Date: ____/____/________

*It is for discipline that you have to endure. God is treating you as sons. For what son is there whom his father does not discipline? If you are left without discipline, in which all have participated, then you are illegitimate children and not sons. Besides this, we have had earthly fathers who disciplined us and we respected them. Shall we not much more be subject to the Father of spirits and live? For they disciplined us for a short time as it seemed best to them, but he disciplines us for our good, that we may share his holiness. For the moment all discipline seems painful rather than pleasant, but later it yields the peaceful fruit of righteousness to those who have been trained by it.*

**Hebrews 12:7-11 (ESV)**

## I am thankful for…

**1)**______________________________

**2)**______________________________

**3)**______________________________

## Scripture Reflection

______________________________

______________________________

______________________________

## Affirmation — I am…

______________________________

______________________________

______________________________

## Personal Notes

______________________________

______________________________

______________________________

______________________________

______________________________

______________________________

______________________________

______________________________

*"I want my life and my marriage to look less like the world and more like Christ."*

**Marquis Clarke**

**Quote Reflection**

______________________________________________

______________________________________________

______________________________________________

**Today was a great day because…**

1)____________________________________________

2)____________________________________________

3)____________________________________________

**I could have made today better by…**

______________________________________________

______________________________________________

______________________________________________

**Personal Notes**

______________________________________________

______________________________________________

______________________________________________

______________________________________________

______________________________________________

______________________________________________

______________________________________________

______________________________________________

Date: ____/____/____

*Discipline your son, for there is hope; do not set your heart on putting him to death. A man of great wrath will pay the penalty, for if you deliver him, you will only have to do it again.*

**Proverbs 19:18-19 (ESV)**

**I am thankful for…**

1)________________________________________

2)________________________________________

3)________________________________________

**Scripture Reflection**

________________________________________

________________________________________

________________________________________

**Affirmation — I am…**

________________________________________

________________________________________

________________________________________

**Personal Notes**

________________________________________

________________________________________

________________________________________

________________________________________

________________________________________

________________________________________

________________________________________

________________________________________

*"The most important thing a father can do for his children is to love their mother."*
**Henry Ward Beecher**

## Quote Reflection

______________________________________________

______________________________________________

______________________________________________

## Today was a great day because…

1)____________________________________________

2)____________________________________________

3)____________________________________________

## I could have made today better by…

______________________________________________

______________________________________________

______________________________________________

## Personal Notes

______________________________________________

______________________________________________

______________________________________________

______________________________________________

______________________________________________

______________________________________________

______________________________________________

______________________________________________

Date: ____/____/____

*Here for the third time I am ready to come to you. And I will not be a burden, for I seek not what is yours but you. For children are not obligated to save up for their parents, but parents for their children.*

**2 Corinthians 12:14 (ESV)**

**I am thankful for…**

**1)**______________________________

**2)**______________________________

**3)**______________________________

**Scripture Reflection**

______________________________

______________________________

______________________________

**Affirmation — I am…**

______________________________

______________________________

______________________________

**Personal Notes**

______________________________

______________________________

______________________________

______________________________

______________________________

______________________________

______________________________

______________________________

*"The man who loves his wife above all else on earth gains the freedom and power to pursue other noble, but lesser, loves."*
**David Jeremiah**

## Quote Reflection

______________________________________________

______________________________________________

______________________________________________

## Today was a great day because…

1)____________________________________________

2)____________________________________________

3)____________________________________________

## I could have made today better by…

______________________________________________

______________________________________________

______________________________________________

## Personal Notes

______________________________________________

______________________________________________

______________________________________________

______________________________________________

______________________________________________

______________________________________________

______________________________________________

______________________________________________

Date: ____/____/____

*And he will go before him in the spirit and power of Elijah, to turn the hearts of the fathers to the children, and the disobedient to the wisdom of the just, to make ready for the Lord a people prepared.*

**Luke 1:17 (ESV)**

**I am thankful for…**

1)____________________

2)____________________

3)____________________

**Scripture Reflection**

**Affirmation — I am…**

**Personal Notes**

*"Men, you'll never be a good groom to your wife unless you're first a good bride to Jesus."*
**Tim Keller**

## Quote Reflection

________________________________________
________________________________________
________________________________________

## Today was a great day because…

**1)**______________________________________
**2)**______________________________________
**3)**______________________________________

## I could have made today better by…

________________________________________
________________________________________
________________________________________

## Personal Notes

________________________________________
________________________________________
________________________________________
________________________________________
________________________________________
________________________________________
________________________________________
________________________________________

Date: ____/____/____

*For I have chosen him, that he may command his children and his household after him to keep the way of the Lord by doing righteousness and justice, so that the Lord may bring to Abraham what he has promised him.*

**Genesis 18:19 (ESV)**

**I am thankful for…**

1)______________________________

2)______________________________

3)______________________________

**Scripture Reflection**

______________________________

______________________________

______________________________

**Affirmation — I am…**

______________________________

______________________________

______________________________

**Personal Notes**

______________________________

______________________________

______________________________

______________________________

______________________________

______________________________

______________________________

______________________________

*"Marriage was ordained for a remedy and to increase the world and for the man to help the woman and the woman the man, with all love and kindness."*

**William Tyndale**

## Quote Reflection

______________________________________________

______________________________________________

______________________________________________

## Today was a great day because…

1)____________________________________________

2)____________________________________________

3)____________________________________________

## I could have made today better by…

______________________________________________

______________________________________________

______________________________________________

## Personal Notes

______________________________________________

______________________________________________

______________________________________________

______________________________________________

______________________________________________

______________________________________________

______________________________________________

______________________________________________

Date: ____/____/________

*He must manage his own household well, with all dignity keeping his children submissive,*

**1 Timothy 3:4 (ESV)**

**I am thankful for…**

1)________________

2)________________

3)________________

**Scripture Reflection**

________________

________________

________________

**Affirmation — I am…**

________________

________________

________________

**Personal Notes**

________________

________________

________________

________________

________________

________________

________________

________________

*"The happiness of married life depends upon making small sacrifices with readiness and cheerfulness."*

**John Selden**

## Quote Reflection

______________________________________________

______________________________________________

______________________________________________

## Today was a great day because…

1)____________________________________________

2)____________________________________________

3)____________________________________________

## I could have made today better by…

______________________________________________

______________________________________________

______________________________________________

## Personal Notes

______________________________________________

______________________________________________

______________________________________________

______________________________________________

______________________________________________

______________________________________________

______________________________________________

______________________________________________

Date: ____/____/____

*How can a young man keep his way pure?*
*By guarding it according to your word.*
**Psalm 119:9 (ESV)**

**I am thankful for…**

**1)**______________________________

**2)**______________________________

**3)**______________________________

**Scripture Reflection**

______________________________

______________________________

______________________________

**Affirmation — I am…**

______________________________

______________________________

______________________________

**Personal Notes**

______________________________

______________________________

______________________________

______________________________

______________________________

______________________________

______________________________

______________________________

*"In sharp contrast with our culture, the Bible teaches that the essence of marriage is a sacrificial commitment to the good of the other. That means that love is more fundamentally action than emotion."*

**Tim Keller**

## Quote Reflection

________________________________________

________________________________________

________________________________________

## Today was a great day because…

**1)**______________________________________

**2)**______________________________________

**3)**______________________________________

## I could have made today better by…

________________________________________

________________________________________

________________________________________

## Personal Notes

________________________________________

________________________________________

________________________________________

________________________________________

________________________________________

________________________________________

________________________________________

________________________________________

Date: ____/____/____

*As a father shows compassion to his children,*
*so the Lord shows compassion to those who fear him.*
**Psalm 103:13 (ESV)**

**I am thankful for…**

1) ____________________

2) ____________________

3) ____________________

**Scripture Reflection**

____________________

____________________

____________________

**Affirmation — I am…**

____________________

____________________

____________________

**Personal Notes**

____________________

____________________

____________________

____________________

____________________

____________________

____________________

____________________

*"If you want something to last forever, you treat it differently. You shield it and protect it. You never abuse it. You don't expose it to the elements. You don't make it common or ordinary. If it ever becomes tarnished, you lovingly polish it until it gleams like new. It becomes special because you have made it so, and it grows more beautiful and precious as time goes by."*

**F. Burton Howard**

## Quote Reflection

___________________________________________

___________________________________________

___________________________________________

## Today was a great day because…

1)_________________________________________

2)_________________________________________

3)_________________________________________

## I could have made today better by…

___________________________________________

___________________________________________

___________________________________________

## Personal Notes

___________________________________________

___________________________________________

___________________________________________

___________________________________________

___________________________________________

___________________________________________

___________________________________________

___________________________________________

Date: ____/____/____

*...if anyone is above reproach, the husband of one wife, and his children are believers and not open to the charge of debauchery or insubordination...*

**Titus 1:6 (ESV)**

## I am thankful for...

**1)**____________________

**2)**____________________

**3)**____________________

## Scripture Reflection

## Affirmation — I am...

## Personal Notes

*"'Being in love' is not merely a feeling. It is a deep unity maintained by the will and deliberately strengthened by habit; reinforced by grace, which both partners ask, and receive from God."*

**C.S. Lewis**

## Quote Reflection

___

___

___

## Today was a great day because…

1)___

2)___

3)___

## I could have made today better by…

___

___

___

## Personal Notes

___

___

___

___

___

___

___

___

Date: ____/____/________

*They shall not labor in vain or bear children for calamity,*
*for they shall be the offspring of the blessed of the Lord,*
*and their descendants with them.*

**Isaiah 65:23 (ESV)**

**I am thankful for…**

1) ________________________________

2) ________________________________

3) ________________________________

**Scripture Reflection**

________________________________

________________________________

________________________________

**Affirmation — I am…**

________________________________

________________________________

________________________________

**Personal Notes**

________________________________

________________________________

________________________________

________________________________

________________________________

________________________________

________________________________

________________________________

*"Consider your spouse in every decision you make, because every decision you make will effect them in some way."*

**Dave Willis**

## Quote Reflection

______________________________________________

______________________________________________

______________________________________________

## Today was a great day because…

1)____________________________________________

2)____________________________________________

3)____________________________________________

## I could have made today better by…

______________________________________________

______________________________________________

______________________________________________

## Personal Notes

______________________________________________

______________________________________________

______________________________________________

______________________________________________

______________________________________________

______________________________________________

______________________________________________

______________________________________________

Date: ____/____/____

*And I declare to him that I am about to punish his house forever, for the iniquity that he knew, because his sons were blaspheming God, and he did not restrain them.*

**1 Samuel 3:13 (ESV)**

## I am thankful for…

1) ______________________________

2) ______________________________

3) ______________________________

## Scripture Reflection

______________________________

______________________________

______________________________

## Affirmation — I am…

______________________________

______________________________

______________________________

## Personal Notes

______________________________

______________________________

______________________________

______________________________

______________________________

______________________________

______________________________

______________________________

*"Great marriages don't happen by luck or by accident. They are the result of a consistent investment of time, thoughtfulness, forgiveness, affection, prayer, mutual respect, and a rock-solid commitment between a husband and a wife."*

**Dave Willis**

## Quote Reflection

___

___

___

## Today was a great day because…

1)___

2)___

3)___

## I could have made today better by…

___

___

___

## Personal Notes

___

___

___

___

___

___

___

___

Date: ____/____/____

*...but whoever causes one of these little ones who believe in me to sin, it would be better for him to have a great millstone fastened around his neck and to be drowned in the depth of the sea.*

**Matthew 18:6 (ESV)**

**I am thankful for...**

1)____________________

2)____________________

3)____________________

**Scripture Reflection**

**Affirmation — I am...**

**Personal Notes**

*"Children are the world's most valuable resource and its best hope for the future."*
**John F. Kennedy**

## Quote Reflection

________________________________________
________________________________________
________________________________________

## Today was a great day because…

**1)**______________________________________
**2)**______________________________________
**3)**______________________________________

## I could have made today better by…

________________________________________
________________________________________
________________________________________

## Personal Notes

________________________________________
________________________________________
________________________________________
________________________________________
________________________________________
________________________________________
________________________________________
________________________________________

Date: ____/____/____

*Listen to your father who gave you life,*
*and do not despise your mother when she is old.*
**Proverbs 23:22 (ESV)**

**I am thankful for…**

1)____________________

2)____________________

3)____________________

**Scripture Reflection**

____________________

____________________

____________________

**Affirmation — I am…**

____________________

____________________

____________________

**Personal Notes**

____________________

____________________

____________________

____________________

____________________

____________________

____________________

____________________

*"Because your children are still your children, your prayers will always have impact on their lives. You may no longer be able to tell them what to do, but you can sure tell the enemy what to do."*
**Stormie Omartain**

## Quote Reflection

______________________________________________

______________________________________________

______________________________________________

## Today was a great day because…

**1)**______________________________________________

**2)**______________________________________________

**3)**______________________________________________

## I could have made today better by…

______________________________________________

______________________________________________

______________________________________________

## Personal Notes

______________________________________________

______________________________________________

______________________________________________

______________________________________________

______________________________________________

______________________________________________

______________________________________________

______________________________________________

Date: ____/____/____

*My son, do not despise the Lord's discipline or be weary of his reproof, for the Lord reproves him whom he loves, as a father the son in whom he delights.*

**Proverbs 3:11-12 (ESV)**

**I am thankful for…**

1)____________________

2)____________________

3)____________________

**Scripture Reflection**

____________________

____________________

____________________

**Affirmation — I am…**

____________________

____________________

____________________

**Personal Notes**

____________________

____________________

____________________

____________________

____________________

____________________

____________________

____________________

*"There can be no keener revelation of a society's soul than the way it treats its children."*

**Nelson Mandela**

## Quote Reflection

______________________________________________

______________________________________________

______________________________________________

## Today was a great day because…

1)____________________________________________

2)____________________________________________

3)____________________________________________

## I could have made today better by…

______________________________________________

______________________________________________

______________________________________________

## Personal Notes

______________________________________________

______________________________________________

______________________________________________

______________________________________________

______________________________________________

______________________________________________

______________________________________________

______________________________________________

Date: ____/____/____

*All Scripture is breathed out by God and profitable for teaching, for reproof, for correction, and for training in righteousness.*

**2 Timothy 3:16 (ESV)**

## I am thankful for…

1)______________________________

2)______________________________

3)______________________________

## Scripture Reflection

______________________________

______________________________

______________________________

## Affirmation — I am…

______________________________

______________________________

______________________________

## Personal Notes

______________________________

______________________________

______________________________

______________________________

______________________________

______________________________

______________________________

______________________________

*"Each we make deposits in the memory banks of our children."*
**Charles R. Swindol**

## Quote Reflection

______________________________________________________________________

______________________________________________________________________

______________________________________________________________________

## Today was a great day because…

1)____________________________________________________________________

2)____________________________________________________________________

3)____________________________________________________________________

## I could have made today better by…

______________________________________________________________________

______________________________________________________________________

______________________________________________________________________

## Personal Notes

______________________________________________________________________

______________________________________________________________________

______________________________________________________________________

______________________________________________________________________

______________________________________________________________________

______________________________________________________________________

______________________________________________________________________

______________________________________________________________________

Date: ____/____/____

*Honor your father and your mother, as the Lord your God commanded you, that your days may be long, and that it may go well with you in the land that the Lord your God is giving you.*
**Deuteronomy 5:16 (ESV)**

**I am thankful for…**

**1)**______________________________

**2)**______________________________

**3)**______________________________

**Scripture Reflection**

______________________________

______________________________

______________________________

**Affirmation — I am…**

______________________________

______________________________

______________________________

**Personal Notes**

______________________________

______________________________

______________________________

______________________________

______________________________

______________________________

______________________________

______________________________

*"Unconditional love is loving your kids for who they are, not for what they do... it isn't something you will achieve every minute of every day. But it is the thought we must hold in our hearts every day."*

**Stephanie Marston**

## Quote Reflection

______________________________________________

______________________________________________

______________________________________________

## Today was a great day because…

1)____________________________________________

2)____________________________________________

3)____________________________________________

## I could have made today better by…

______________________________________________

______________________________________________

______________________________________________

## Personal Notes

______________________________________________

______________________________________________

______________________________________________

______________________________________________

______________________________________________

______________________________________________

______________________________________________

______________________________________________

Date: ____/____/________

*So Jesus said to them, "Truly, truly, I say to you, the Son can do nothing of his own accord, but only what he sees the Father doing. For whatever the Father does, that the Son does likewise.*

**John 5:19 (ESV)**

**I am thankful for…**

1)________________________________

2)________________________________

3)________________________________

**Scripture Reflection**

________________________________

________________________________

________________________________

**Affirmation — I am…**

________________________________

________________________________

________________________________

**Personal Notes**

________________________________

________________________________

________________________________

________________________________

________________________________

________________________________

________________________________

________________________________

*"Families are messy. Immortal families are eternally messy. Sometimes the best we can do is to remind each other that we're related for better or for worse...and try to keep the maiming and killing to a minimum."*
**Rick Riordan**

## Quote Reflection

________________________________________

________________________________________

________________________________________

## Today was a great day because...

**1)**______________________________________

**2)**______________________________________

**3)**______________________________________

## I could have made today better by...

________________________________________

________________________________________

________________________________________

## Personal Notes

________________________________________

________________________________________

________________________________________

________________________________________

________________________________________

________________________________________

________________________________________

________________________________________

Date: ____/____/____

*The Father loves the Son and has given all things into his hand.*

**John 3:35 (ESV)**

**I am thankful for…**

**1)**______________________________

**2)**______________________________

**3)**______________________________

**Scripture Reflection**

______________________________

______________________________

______________________________

**Affirmation — I am…**

______________________________

______________________________

______________________________

**Personal Notes**

______________________________

______________________________

______________________________

______________________________

______________________________

______________________________

______________________________

______________________________

*"Being a family means you are a part of something very wonderful. It means you will love and be loved for the rest of your life."*
**Lisa Weedn**

## Quote Reflection

________________________________

________________________________

________________________________

## Today was a great day because…

1)________________________________

2)________________________________

3)________________________________

## I could have made today better by…

________________________________

________________________________

________________________________

## Personal Notes

________________________________

________________________________

________________________________

________________________________

________________________________

________________________________

________________________________

________________________________

Date: ____/____/____

*Behold, everyone who uses proverbs will use this proverb about you: 'Like mother, like daughter.'*

**Ezekiel 16:44 (ESV)**

## I am thankful for…

1) ____________________

2) ____________________

3) ____________________

## Scripture Reflection

____________________

____________________

____________________

## Affirmation — I am…

____________________

____________________

____________________

## Personal Notes

____________________

____________________

____________________

____________________

____________________

____________________

____________________

____________________

*"There is no doubt that it is around the family and the home that all the greatest virtues, the most dominating virtues of humans, are created, strengthened and maintained."*

**Winston Churchill**

## Quote Reflection

______________________________________________

______________________________________________

______________________________________________

## Today was a great day because…

1)____________________________________________

2)____________________________________________

3)____________________________________________

## I could have made today better by…

______________________________________________

______________________________________________

______________________________________________

## Personal Notes

______________________________________________

______________________________________________

______________________________________________

______________________________________________

______________________________________________

______________________________________________

______________________________________________

______________________________________________

Date: ______ / ______ / ______

*If one curses his father or his mother,*
*his lamp will be put out in utter darkness.*
**Proverbs 20:20 (ESV)**

**I am thankful for…**

1) ____________________

2) ____________________

3) ____________________

**Scripture Reflection**

____________________

____________________

____________________

**Affirmation — I am…**

____________________

____________________

____________________

**Personal Notes**

____________________

____________________

____________________

____________________

____________________

____________________

____________________

____________________

*"Children are likely to live up to what you believe of them."*

**Lady Bird Johnson**

## Quote Reflection

______________________________________________

______________________________________________

______________________________________________

## Today was a great day because…

1)____________________________________________

2)____________________________________________

3)____________________________________________

## I could have made today better by…

______________________________________________

______________________________________________

______________________________________________

## Personal Notes

______________________________________________

______________________________________________

______________________________________________

______________________________________________

______________________________________________

______________________________________________

______________________________________________

______________________________________________

Date:______/______/______

*I am reminded of your sincere faith, a faith that dwelt first in your grandmother Lois and your mother Eunice and now, I am sure, dwells in you as well.*

**2 Timothy 1:5 (ESV)**

## I am thankful for…

1)________________________________________

2)________________________________________

3)________________________________________

## Scripture Reflection

## Affirmation — I am…

## Personal Notes

*"The greatest legacy one can pass on to one's children and grandchildren is not money or other material things accumulated in one's life, but rather a legacy of character and faith."*
**Billy Graham**

## Quote Reflection

______________________________

______________________________

______________________________

## Today was a great day because…

1)______________________________

2)______________________________

3)______________________________

## I could have made today better by…

______________________________

______________________________

______________________________

## Personal Notes

______________________________

______________________________

______________________________

______________________________

______________________________

______________________________

______________________________

______________________________

Date: ____/____/________

*For God commanded, 'Honor your father and your mother,' and, 'Whoever reviles father or mother must surely die.' But you say, 'If anyone tells his father or his mother, "What you would have gained from me is given to God," he need not honor his father.' So for the sake of your tradition you have made void the word of God.*

**Matthew 15:4-6 (ESV)**

**I am thankful for…**

**1)**________________________________________

**2)**________________________________________

**3)**________________________________________

**Scripture Reflection**

________________________________________

________________________________________

________________________________________

**Affirmation — I am…**

________________________________________

________________________________________

________________________________________

**Personal Notes**

________________________________________

________________________________________

________________________________________

________________________________________

________________________________________

________________________________________

________________________________________

________________________________________

*"We worry about what a child will become tomorrow, yet we forget that he is someone today."*
**Stacia Tauscher**

**Quote Reflection**

______________________________

______________________________

______________________________

**Today was a great day because…**

1)______________________________

2)______________________________

3)______________________________

**I could have made today better by…**

______________________________

______________________________

______________________________

**Personal Notes**

______________________________

______________________________

______________________________

______________________________

______________________________

______________________________

______________________________

______________________________

Date: ____/____/____

*As one whom his mother comforts, so I will comfort you;*
*you shall be comforted in Jerusalem.*
**Isaiah 66:13 (ESV)**

## I am thankful for…

1) ____________________
2) ____________________
3) ____________________

## Scripture Reflection

____________________
____________________
____________________

## Affirmation — I am…

____________________
____________________
____________________

## Personal Notes

____________________
____________________
____________________
____________________
____________________
____________________
____________________
____________________

*"Children are not things to be molded,*
*but are people to be unfolded."*
**Jess Lair**

**Quote Reflection**

______________________________________________

______________________________________________

______________________________________________

**Today was a great day because…**

1)____________________________________________

2)____________________________________________

3)____________________________________________

**I could have made today better by…**

______________________________________________

______________________________________________

______________________________________________

**Personal Notes**

______________________________________________

______________________________________________

______________________________________________

______________________________________________

______________________________________________

______________________________________________

______________________________________________

______________________________________________

Date: ____/____/____

*For you formed my inward parts;*
*you knitted me together in my mother's womb.*
**Psalm 139:13 (ESV)**

## I am thankful for…

**1)**______________________________
**2)**______________________________
**3)**______________________________

## Scripture Reflection

______________________________
______________________________
______________________________

## Affirmation — I am…

______________________________
______________________________
______________________________

## Personal Notes

______________________________
______________________________
______________________________
______________________________
______________________________
______________________________
______________________________
______________________________

*"Children need models rather than critics."*

**Joseph Joubert**

## Quote Reflection

____________________________________________________________

____________________________________________________________

____________________________________________________________

## Today was a great day because…

**1)**__________________________________________________________

**2)**__________________________________________________________

**3)**__________________________________________________________

## I could have made today better by…

____________________________________________________________

____________________________________________________________

____________________________________________________________

## Personal Notes

____________________________________________________________

____________________________________________________________

____________________________________________________________

____________________________________________________________

____________________________________________________________

____________________________________________________________

____________________________________________________________

____________________________________________________________

Date: ____/____/________

*When a woman is giving birth, she has sorrow because her hour has come, but when she has delivered the baby, she no longer remembers the anguish, for joy that a human being has been born into the world.*

**John 16:21 (ESV)**

**I am thankful for…**

1) ______________________________

2) ______________________________

3) ______________________________

**Scripture Reflection**

______________________________

______________________________

______________________________

**Affirmation — I am…**

______________________________

______________________________

______________________________

**Personal Notes**

______________________________

______________________________

______________________________

______________________________

______________________________

______________________________

______________________________

______________________________

*"Children have never been very good at listening to their elders, but they have never failed to imitate them."*
**James Baldwin**

## Quote Reflection

______________________________________________

______________________________________________

______________________________________________

## Today was a great day because…

1)____________________________________________

2)____________________________________________

3)____________________________________________

## I could have made today better by…

______________________________________________

______________________________________________

______________________________________________

## Personal Notes

______________________________________________

______________________________________________

______________________________________________

______________________________________________

______________________________________________

______________________________________________

______________________________________________

______________________________________________

Date: ____/____/____

*A gracious woman gets honor, and violent men get riches.*

**Proverbs 11:16 (ESV)**

## I am thankful for…

1)____________________

2)____________________

3)____________________

## Scripture Reflection

____________________

____________________

____________________

## Affirmation — I am…

____________________

____________________

____________________

## Personal Notes

____________________

____________________

____________________

____________________

____________________

____________________

____________________

____________________

*"Children are like wet cement.*
*Whatever falls on them makes an impression."*
**Haim Ginott**

## Quote Reflection

______________________________________________

______________________________________________

______________________________________________

## Today was a great day because…

1)____________________________________________

2)____________________________________________

3)____________________________________________

## I could have made today better by…

______________________________________________

______________________________________________

______________________________________________

## Personal Notes

______________________________________________

______________________________________________

______________________________________________

______________________________________________

______________________________________________

______________________________________________

______________________________________________

______________________________________________

Date: ____/____/____

*My son, keep your father's commandment,*
*and forsake not your mother's teaching.*
*Bind them on your heart always;*
*tie them around your neck.*
**Proverbs 6:20-21 (ESV)**

**I am thankful for…**

1) ______________________
2) ______________________
3) ______________________

**Scripture Reflection**

______________________
______________________
______________________

**Affirmation — I am…**

______________________
______________________
______________________

**Personal Notes**

______________________
______________________
______________________
______________________
______________________
______________________
______________________
______________________

*"You have to love your children unselfishly.*
*That is hard. But it is the only way."*
**Barbara Bush**

## Quote Reflection

________________________________________

________________________________________

________________________________________

## Today was a great day because…

1)______________________________________

2)______________________________________

3)______________________________________

## I could have made today better by…

________________________________________

________________________________________

________________________________________

## Personal Notes

________________________________________

________________________________________

________________________________________

________________________________________

________________________________________

________________________________________

________________________________________

________________________________________

Date: ____/____/____

*Whoever troubles his own household will inherit*
*the wind, and the fool will be servant to the wise of heart.*
**Proverbs 11:29 (ESV)**

**I am thankful for…**

1)____________________

2)____________________

3)____________________

**Scripture Reflection**

____________________

____________________

____________________

**Affirmation — I am…**

____________________

____________________

____________________

**Personal Notes**

____________________

____________________

____________________

____________________

____________________

____________________

____________________

____________________

*"The potential possibilities of any child are the most intriguing and stimulating in all creation."*

**Ray L. Wilbur**

## Quote Reflection

______________________________________________

______________________________________________

______________________________________________

## Today was a great day because…

1)____________________________________________

2)____________________________________________

3)____________________________________________

## I could have made today better by…

______________________________________________

______________________________________________

______________________________________________

## Personal Notes

______________________________________________

______________________________________________

______________________________________________

______________________________________________

______________________________________________

______________________________________________

______________________________________________

______________________________________________

Date: ____/____/____

*However, let each one of you love his wife as himself, and let the wife see that she respects her husband.*
**Ephesians 5:33 (ESV)**

## I am thankful for…

1) ____________________
2) ____________________
3) ____________________

## Scripture Reflection

____________________
____________________
____________________

## Affirmation — I am…

____________________
____________________
____________________

## Personal Notes

____________________
____________________
____________________
____________________
____________________
____________________
____________________
____________________

*"Children are the living messages we send to a time we will not see."*
**John F. Kennedy**

**Quote Reflection**

______________________________

______________________________

______________________________

**Today was a great day because…**

1)______________________________

2)______________________________

3)______________________________

**I could have made today better by…**

______________________________

______________________________

______________________________

**Personal Notes**

______________________________

______________________________

______________________________

______________________________

______________________________

______________________________

______________________________

______________________________

Date: ____/____/____

*And I say to you: whoever divorces his wife, except for sexual immorality, and marries another, commits adultery."*

**Matthew 19:9 (ESV)**

## I am thankful for…

1) ____________________

2) ____________________

3) ____________________

## Scripture Reflection

____________________

____________________

____________________

## Affirmation — I am…

____________________

____________________

____________________

## Personal Notes

____________________

____________________

____________________

____________________

____________________

____________________

____________________

____________________

*"Don't worry that children never listen to you; worry that they are always watching you."*
**Robert Fulghum**

## Quote Reflection

______________________________________________

______________________________________________

______________________________________________

## Today was a great day because…

1)____________________________________________

2)____________________________________________

3)____________________________________________

## I could have made today better by…

______________________________________________

______________________________________________

______________________________________________

## Personal Notes

______________________________________________

______________________________________________

______________________________________________

______________________________________________

______________________________________________

______________________________________________

______________________________________________

______________________________________________

Date: ____/____/____

*And above all these put on love, which binds everything together in perfect harmony.*

**Colossians 3:14 (ESV)**

## I am thankful for…

1) ____________________

2) ____________________

3) ____________________

## Scripture Reflection

____________________

____________________

____________________

## Affirmation — I am…

____________________

____________________

____________________

## Personal Notes

____________________

____________________

____________________

____________________

____________________

____________________

____________________

____________________

*"The greatest gifts you can give your children are the roots of responsibility and the wings of independence."*
**Denis Waitley**

## Quote Reflection

______________________________________________

______________________________________________

______________________________________________

## Today was a great day because…

**1)**______________________________________________

**2)**______________________________________________

**3)**______________________________________________

## I could have made today better by…

______________________________________________

______________________________________________

______________________________________________

## Personal Notes

______________________________________________

______________________________________________

______________________________________________

______________________________________________

______________________________________________

______________________________________________

______________________________________________

______________________________________________

Date: ____/____/____

*Let a woman learn quietly with all submissiveness. I do not permit a woman to teach or to exercise authority over a man; rather, she is to remain quiet. For Adam was formed first, then Eve; and Adam was not deceived, but the woman was deceived and became a transgressor. Yet she will be saved through childbearing—if they continue in faith and love and holiness, with self-control.*

**1 Timothy 2:11-15 (ESV)**

## I am thankful for…

1) ______________________

2) ______________________

3) ______________________

## Scripture Reflection

______________________

______________________

______________________

## Affirmation — I am…

______________________

______________________

______________________

## Personal Notes

______________________

______________________

______________________

______________________

______________________

______________________

______________________

______________________

*"Children aren't coloring books.*
*You don't get to fill them with your favorite colors."*
**Khaled Hosseini**

## Quote Reflection

______________________________________________

______________________________________________

______________________________________________

## Today was a great day because…

1)____________________________________________

2)____________________________________________

3)____________________________________________

## I could have made today better by…

______________________________________________

______________________________________________

______________________________________________

## Personal Notes

______________________________________________

______________________________________________

______________________________________________

______________________________________________

______________________________________________

______________________________________________

______________________________________________

______________________________________________

Date: ____/____/____

*Older women likewise are to be reverent in behavior,*
*not slanderers or slaves to much wine.*
**Titus 2:3 (ESV)**

**I am thankful for…**

1)______________________________

2)______________________________

3)______________________________

**Scripture Reflection**

______________________________

______________________________

______________________________

**Affirmation — I am…**

______________________________

______________________________

______________________________

**Personal Notes**

______________________________

______________________________

______________________________

______________________________

______________________________

______________________________

______________________________

______________________________

*"Don't handicap your children by making their lives easy."*
**Robert A. Heinlein**

## Quote Reflection

______________________________________________

______________________________________________

______________________________________________

## Today was a great day because…

1)____________________________________________

2)____________________________________________

3)____________________________________________

## I could have made today better by…

______________________________________________

______________________________________________

______________________________________________

## Personal Notes

______________________________________________

______________________________________________

______________________________________________

______________________________________________

______________________________________________

______________________________________________

______________________________________________

______________________________________________

Date: ____/____/____

*Do not rebuke an older man but encourage him as you would a father, younger men as brothers, older women as mothers, younger women as sisters, in all purity.*

**1 Timothy 5:1-2 (ESV)**

## I am thankful for…

**1)** ______________________

**2)** ______________________

**3)** ______________________

## Scripture Reflection

______________________

______________________

______________________

## Affirmation — I am…

______________________

______________________

______________________

## Personal Notes

______________________

______________________

______________________

______________________

______________________

______________________

______________________

______________________

*"Your children are the greatest gift God will give to you, and their souls the heaviest responsibility He will place in your hands. Take time with them, teach them to have faith in God. Be a person in whom they can have faith. When you are old, nothing else you've done will have mattered as much."*

**Lisa Wingate**

## Quote Reflection

______________________________

______________________________

______________________________

## Today was a great day because…

1)______________________________

2)______________________________

3)______________________________

## I could have made today better by…

______________________________

______________________________

______________________________

## Personal Notes

______________________________

______________________________

______________________________

______________________________

______________________________

______________________________

______________________________

______________________________

Date: ____/____/____

*Nevertheless, in the Lord woman is not independent of man nor man of woman;*

**1 Corinthians 11:11 (ESV)**

**I am thankful for…**

1)________________________________________

2)________________________________________

3)________________________________________

**Scripture Reflection**

________________________________________

________________________________________

________________________________________

**Affirmation — I am…**

________________________________________

________________________________________

________________________________________

**Personal Notes**

________________________________________

________________________________________

________________________________________

________________________________________

________________________________________

________________________________________

________________________________________

________________________________________

*"I think that the best thing we can do for our children is to allow them to do things for themselves, allow them to be strong, allow them to experience life on their own terms, allow them to take the subway... let them be better people, let them believe more in themselves."*

**C. JoyBell C.**

## Quote Reflection

______________________________________________

______________________________________________

______________________________________________

## Today was a great day because…

1)____________________________________________

2)____________________________________________

3)____________________________________________

## I could have made today better by…

______________________________________________

______________________________________________

______________________________________________

## Personal Notes

______________________________________________

______________________________________________

______________________________________________

______________________________________________

______________________________________________

______________________________________________

______________________________________________

______________________________________________

Date: ____/____/____

*Their wives likewise must be dignified, not slanderers, but sober-minded, faithful in all things.*

**1 Timothy 3:11 (ESV)**

## I am thankful for…

1) ______________________________

2) ______________________________

3) ______________________________

## Scripture Reflection

______________________________

______________________________

______________________________

## Affirmation — I am…

______________________________

______________________________

______________________________

## Personal Notes

______________________________

______________________________

______________________________

______________________________

______________________________

______________________________

______________________________

______________________________

*"What children need most are the essentials that grandparents provide in abundance. They give unconditional love, kindness, patience, humor, comfort, lessons in life. And, most importantly, cookies."*
**Rudolph Giuliani**

## Quote Reflection

___

___

___

## Today was a great day because…

1)___

2)___

3)___

## I could have made today better by…

___

___

___

## Personal Notes

___

___

___

___

___

___

___

___

Date: ____/____/____

*A foolish son is ruin to his father,*
*and a wife's quarreling is a continual dripping of rain.*
**Proverbs 19:13 (ESV)**

**I am thankful for…**

**1)**______________________________

**2)**______________________________

**3)**______________________________

**Scripture Reflection**

______________________________

______________________________

______________________________

**Affirmation — I am…**

______________________________

______________________________

______________________________

**Personal Notes**

______________________________

______________________________

______________________________

______________________________

______________________________

______________________________

______________________________

______________________________

*"A Grandmother thinks of her grandchildren day and night, even when they are not with her. She will always love them more than anyone would understand."*

**Karen Gibbs**

## Quote Reflection

______________________________________________

______________________________________________

______________________________________________

## Today was a great day because…

1)____________________________________________

2)____________________________________________

3)____________________________________________

## I could have made today better by…

______________________________________________

______________________________________________

______________________________________________

## Personal Notes

______________________________________________

______________________________________________

______________________________________________

______________________________________________

______________________________________________

______________________________________________

______________________________________________

______________________________________________

Date: ____/____/____

*But if serving the LORD seems undesirable to you, then choose for yourselves this day whom you will serve, whether the gods your ancestors served beyond the Euphrates, or the gods of the Amorites, in whose land you are living. But as for me and my household, we will serve the LORD.*

**Joshua 24:15 (NIV)**

**I am thankful for…**

**1)**______________________________

**2)**______________________________

**3)**______________________________

**Scripture Reflection**

______________________________

______________________________

______________________________

**Affirmation — I am…**

______________________________

______________________________

______________________________

**Personal Notes**

______________________________

______________________________

______________________________

______________________________

______________________________

______________________________

______________________________

______________________________

*"Grandparents are extremely rich folks
with silver in their hair and gold in their hearts."*
**Mamur Mustapha**

## Quote Reflection

___

___

___

## Today was a great day because…

1)___

2)___

3)___

## I could have made today better by…

___

___

___

## Personal Notes

___

___

___

___

___

___

___

___

Date: ____/____/____

*Love is patient, love is kind. It does not envy, it does not boast,*
*it is not proud. It does not dishonor others, it is not self-seeking,*
*it is not easily angered, it keeps no record of wrongs.*
*Love does not delight in evil but rejoices with the truth.*
*It always protects, always trusts, always hopes, always perseveres.*

**1 Corinthians 13:4-7 (NIV)**

## I am thankful for…

**1)**______________________________

**2)**______________________________

**3)**______________________________

## Scripture Reflection

______________________________

______________________________

______________________________

## Affirmation — I am…

______________________________

______________________________

______________________________

## Personal Notes

______________________________

______________________________

______________________________

______________________________

______________________________

______________________________

______________________________

______________________________

*"A journey is like marriage. The certain way to be wrong is to think you control it."*

**John Steinbeck**

## Quote Reflection

______________________________________________

______________________________________________

______________________________________________

## Today was a great day because…

1)____________________________________________

2)____________________________________________

3)____________________________________________

## I could have made today better by…

______________________________________________

______________________________________________

______________________________________________

## Personal Notes

______________________________________________

______________________________________________

______________________________________________

______________________________________________

______________________________________________

______________________________________________

______________________________________________

______________________________________________

Date: ____/____/____

*The greedy bring ruin to their households,*
*but the one who hates bribes will live.*
**Proverbs 15:27 (NIV)**

## I am thankful for…

1) ______________________________
2) ______________________________
3) ______________________________

## Scripture Reflection

______________________________
______________________________
______________________________

## Affirmation — I am…

______________________________
______________________________
______________________________

## Personal Notes

______________________________
______________________________
______________________________
______________________________
______________________________
______________________________
______________________________
______________________________

*"Before I got married I had six theories about raising children; now, I have six children and no theories."*

**John Wilmot**

## Quote Reflection

______________________________________________

______________________________________________

______________________________________________

## Today was a great day because…

1)____________________________________________

2)____________________________________________

3)____________________________________________

## I could have made today better by…

______________________________________________

______________________________________________

______________________________________________

## Personal Notes

______________________________________________

______________________________________________

______________________________________________

______________________________________________

______________________________________________

______________________________________________

______________________________________________

______________________________________________

Date: ____/____/____

*She gets up while it is still night; she provides food for her family and portions for her female servants. She considers a field and buys it; out of her earnings she plants a vineyard. She sets about her work vigorously; her arms are strong for her tasks.*

**Proverbs 31:15-17 (NIV)**

## I am thankful for…

1) ______________________________
2) ______________________________
3) ______________________________

## Scripture Reflection

______________________________
______________________________
______________________________

## Affirmation — I am…

______________________________
______________________________
______________________________

## Personal Notes

______________________________
______________________________
______________________________
______________________________
______________________________
______________________________
______________________________
______________________________

*"To keep your marriage brimming, with love in the wedding cup, whenever you're wrong, admit it; whenever you're right, shut up."*

**Ogden Nash**

## Quote Reflection

______________________________________________

______________________________________________

______________________________________________

## Today was a great day because…

1)____________________________________________

2)____________________________________________

3)____________________________________________

## I could have made today better by…

______________________________________________

______________________________________________

______________________________________________

## Personal Notes

______________________________________________

______________________________________________

______________________________________________

______________________________________________

______________________________________________

______________________________________________

______________________________________________

______________________________________________

Date: ______/______/______

*Enjoy life with your wife, whom you love, all the days of this meaningless life that God has given you under the sun — all your meaningless days. For this is your lot in life and in your toilsome labor under the sun.*

**Ecclesiastes 9:9 (NIV)**

**I am thankful for…**

1)________________________________________

2)________________________________________

3)________________________________________

**Scripture Reflection**

**Affirmation — I am…**

**Personal Notes**

*"Love is a commitment that will be tested in the most vulnerable areas of spirituality, a commitment that will force you to make some very difficult choices. It is a commitment that demands that you deal with your lust, your greed, your pride, your power, your desire to control, your temper, your patience, and every area of temptation that the Bible clearly talks about. It demands the quality of commitment that Jesus demonstrates in His relationship to us."*

**Ravi Zacharias**

## Quote Reflection

______________________________

______________________________

______________________________

## Today was a great day because…

1)______________________________

2)______________________________

3)______________________________

## I could have made today better by…

______________________________

______________________________

______________________________

## Personal Notes

______________________________

______________________________

______________________________

______________________________

______________________________

______________________________

______________________________

______________________________

Date: ____/____/____

*Though one may be overpowered, two can defend themselves. A cord of three strands is not quickly broken.*
**Ecclesiastes 4:12 (NIV)**

**I am thankful for…**

1)____________________

2)____________________

3)____________________

**Scripture Reflection**

**Affirmation — I am…**

**Personal Notes**

*"The foundation that my parents and grandparents instilled in me is unyielding, especially the principle that teaches me to keep God first in all I do."*

**Carlos Wallace**

## Quote Reflection

______________________________________________

______________________________________________

______________________________________________

## Today was a great day because…

1)____________________________________________

2)____________________________________________

3)____________________________________________

## I could have made today better by…

______________________________________________

______________________________________________

______________________________________________

## Personal Notes

______________________________________________

______________________________________________

______________________________________________

______________________________________________

______________________________________________

______________________________________________

______________________________________________

______________________________________________

Date: ____/____/____

*Be completely humble and gentle; Be patient,*
*bearing with one another in love. Make every effort*
*to keep the unity of the spirit through the bond of peace.*
**Ephesians 4:2-3 (NIV)**

**I am thankful for…**

1)____________________

2)____________________

3)____________________

**Scripture Reflection**

**Affirmation — I am…**

**Personal Notes**

*"We cannot always build the future for our youth,*
*but we can build our youth for the future."*
**Franklin D. Roosevelt**

## Quote Reflection

______________________________________________

______________________________________________

______________________________________________

## Today was a great day because…

1)____________________________________________

2)____________________________________________

3)____________________________________________

## I could have made today better by…

______________________________________________

______________________________________________

______________________________________________

## Personal Notes

______________________________________________

______________________________________________

______________________________________________

______________________________________________

______________________________________________

______________________________________________

______________________________________________

______________________________________________

Date: ____/____/____

*And be kind to one another, tenderhearted, forgiving one another, even as God in Christ forgave you.*
**Ephesians 4:32 (NKJV)**

**I am thankful for…**

**1)**______________________________

**2)**______________________________

**3)**______________________________

**Scripture Reflection**

______________________________

______________________________

______________________________

**Affirmation — I am…**

______________________________

______________________________

______________________________

**Personal Notes**

______________________________

______________________________

______________________________

______________________________

______________________________

______________________________

______________________________

______________________________

*"Our children are only as brilliant as we allow them to be."*

**Eric Michael Leventhal**

## Quote Reflection

______________________________________________

______________________________________________

______________________________________________

## Today was a great day because…

1)____________________________________________

2)____________________________________________

3)____________________________________________

## I could have made today better by…

______________________________________________

______________________________________________

______________________________________________

## Personal Notes

______________________________________________

______________________________________________

______________________________________________

______________________________________________

______________________________________________

______________________________________________

______________________________________________

______________________________________________

Date: ____/____/____

*Marriage should be honored by all,*
*and let the marriage bed be kept pure, for God*
*will judge the adulterer and all the sexually immoral.*
**Hebrews 13:4 (NIV)**

**I am thankful for…**

1) ____________________

2) ____________________

3) ____________________

**Scripture Reflection**

____________________

____________________

____________________

**Affirmation — I am…**

____________________

____________________

____________________

**Personal Notes**

____________________

____________________

____________________

____________________

____________________

____________________

____________________

____________________

*"Parenthood ... It's about guiding the next generation, and forgiving the last."*
**Peter Krause**

## Quote Reflection

______________________________

______________________________

______________________________

## Today was a great day because…

1)______________________________

2)______________________________

3)______________________________

## I could have made today better by…

______________________________

______________________________

______________________________

## Personal Notes

______________________________

______________________________

______________________________

______________________________

______________________________

______________________________

______________________________

______________________________

Date: ____/____/____

*I was young and now I am old, yet I have never seen the righteous forsaken or their children begging bread.*
**Psalms 37:25 (NIV)**

**I am thankful for…**

1)______________________________

2)______________________________

3)______________________________

**Scripture Reflection**

______________________________

______________________________

______________________________

**Affirmation — I am…**

______________________________

______________________________

______________________________

**Personal Notes**

______________________________

______________________________

______________________________

______________________________

______________________________

______________________________

______________________________

______________________________

*"Nobody can do for little children what grandparents do. Grandparents sort of sprinkle stardust over the lives of little children."*

**Alex Haley**

## Quote Reflection

______________________________

______________________________

______________________________

## Today was a great day because…

1)______________________________

2)______________________________

3)______________________________

## I could have made today better by…

______________________________

______________________________

______________________________

## Personal Notes

______________________________

______________________________

______________________________

______________________________

______________________________

______________________________

______________________________

______________________________

“Thoughts disentangle themselves as they pass through the lips and pencil tips.”

*Michael Hyatt*

You are awesome! You've just completed 100 days of journaling.

By now, you've developed a healthy routine of journaling.

You've purposefully dwelt on that which is true, honorable, just, pure, lovely, commendable, excellent, and praiseworthy about your family (Philippians 4:8). Your intentional acts of gratitude have formed a more positive view of your family relationships.

Your reflections on Scripture and meaningful quotes has likely been a rollercoaster ride. From joy-filled Psalms to encouraging wisdom in Proverbs to the convicting words of Jesus, your reflections have begun to influence your actions.

Your affirmations are empowering you to overcome your fears. Many of these fears have hindered deeper relationships in your family.

Take this moment to celebrate your accomplishment of completing 100 days of journaling and celebrate the thriving family relationships you are establishing.

You are well on your way to a wonderful family legacy.

I would love to hear of your experience with the journal. How have your journaling efforts changed your family relationships? Shoot me an email at feedback@MichaelTanner.org.

Date: ____/____/____

*But from everlasting to everlasting the LORD's love is with those who fear him, and his righteousness with their children's children.*
**Psalm 103:17 (NIV)**

**I am thankful for…**

1)____________________

2)____________________

3)____________________

**Scripture Reflection**

____________________

____________________

____________________

**Affirmation — I am…**

____________________

____________________

____________________

**Personal Notes**

____________________

____________________

____________________

____________________

____________________

____________________

____________________

____________________

*"We find delight in the beauty and happiness of children that makes the heart too big for the body."*

**Ralph Waldo Emerson**

**Quote Reflection**

______________________________________________

______________________________________________

______________________________________________

**Today was a great day because…**

1)____________________________________________

2)____________________________________________

3)____________________________________________

**I could have made today better by…**

______________________________________________

______________________________________________

______________________________________________

**Personal Notes**

______________________________________________

______________________________________________

______________________________________________

______________________________________________

______________________________________________

______________________________________________

______________________________________________

______________________________________________

Date: ____/____/____

*But now, O Lord, you are our Father; we are the clay, and you are our potter; we are all the work of your hand.*

**Isaiah 64:8 (ESV)**

## I am thankful for…

1)____________________

2)____________________

3)____________________

## Scripture Reflection

## Affirmation — I am…

## Personal Notes

*"Oh, brothers and sisters, families can be forever! Do not let the lures [or the irritants] of the moment draw you away from them! Divinity, eternity, and family—they go together, hand in hand, and so must we!"*

**Spencer W. Kimball**

## Quote Reflection

______________________________

______________________________

______________________________

## Today was a great day because…

1)______________________________

2)______________________________

3)______________________________

## I could have made today better by…

______________________________

______________________________

______________________________

## Personal Notes

______________________________

______________________________

______________________________

______________________________

______________________________

______________________________

______________________________

______________________________

Date: ____/____/____

*As the Father has loved me, so have I loved you. Abide in my love.*
**John 15:9 (ESV)**

**I am thankful for…**

**1)**______________________________
**2)**______________________________
**3)**______________________________

**Scripture Reflection**

______________________________
______________________________
______________________________

**Affirmation — I am…**

______________________________
______________________________
______________________________

**Personal Notes**

______________________________
______________________________
______________________________
______________________________
______________________________
______________________________
______________________________
______________________________

*"There really are places in the heart you don't even know exist until you love a child."*

**Anne Lamott**

## Quote Reflection

______________________________

______________________________

______________________________

## Today was a great day because…

1)______________________________

2)______________________________

3)______________________________

## I could have made today better by…

______________________________

______________________________

______________________________

## Personal Notes

______________________________

______________________________

______________________________

______________________________

______________________________

______________________________

______________________________

______________________________

Date: ____/____/____

*But you, O Lord, are a God merciful and gracious,*
*slow to anger and abounding in steadfast love and faithfulness.*
**Psalm 86:15 (ESV)**

**I am thankful for…**

1)________________________________

2)________________________________

3)________________________________

**Scripture Reflection**

**Affirmation — I am…**

**Personal Notes**

*"A great marriage is not when the 'perfect couple' comes together. It is when an imperfect couple learns to enjoy their differences."*

**Dave Meurer**

## Quote Reflection

________________________________________

________________________________________

________________________________________

## Today was a great day because…

1)______________________________________

2)______________________________________

3)______________________________________

## I could have made today better by…

________________________________________

________________________________________

________________________________________

## Personal Notes

________________________________________

________________________________________

________________________________________

________________________________________

________________________________________

________________________________________

________________________________________

________________________________________

Date: ____/____/____

*Give thanks to the God of heaven,*
*for his steadfast love endures forever.*
**Psalm 136:26 (ESV)**

## I am thankful for…

1) ______________________________
2) ______________________________
3) ______________________________

## Scripture Reflection

______________________________
______________________________
______________________________

## Affirmation — I am…

______________________________
______________________________
______________________________

## Personal Notes

______________________________
______________________________
______________________________
______________________________
______________________________
______________________________
______________________________
______________________________

*"What is it about grandparents that is so lovely?*
*I'd like to say that grandparents are God's gifts to children.*
*And if they can but see, hear and feel what these people*
*have to give, they can mature at a fast rate."*

**Bill Cosby**

## Quote Reflection

______________________________________________

______________________________________________

______________________________________________

## Today was a great day because…

1)____________________________________________

2)____________________________________________

3)____________________________________________

## I could have made today better by…

______________________________________________

______________________________________________

______________________________________________

## Personal Notes

______________________________________________

______________________________________________

______________________________________________

______________________________________________

______________________________________________

______________________________________________

______________________________________________

______________________________________________

Date: ____/____/____

*But God, being rich in mercy, because of the great love with which he loved us, even when we were dead in our trespasses, made us alive together with Christ — by grace you have been saved — and raised us up with him and seated us with him in the heavenly places in Christ Jesus, so that in the coming ages he might show the immeasurable riches of his grace in kindness toward us in Christ Jesus.*

**Ephesians 2:4-7 (ESV)**

## I am thankful for…

1)________________________________

2)________________________________

3)________________________________

## Scripture Reflection

## Affirmation — I am…

## Personal Notes

*"You don't really understand human nature unless you know why a child on a merry-go-round will wave at his parents every time around — and why his parents will always wave back."*
**William D. Tammeus**

## Quote Reflection

______________________________________________

______________________________________________

______________________________________________

## Today was a great day because…

1)____________________________________________

2)____________________________________________

3)____________________________________________

## I could have made today better by…

______________________________________________

______________________________________________

______________________________________________

## Personal Notes

______________________________________________

______________________________________________

______________________________________________

______________________________________________

______________________________________________

______________________________________________

______________________________________________

______________________________________________

Date: ____/____/________

*How precious is your steadfast love, O God!*
*The children of mankind take refuge in the shadow of your wings.*
**Psalm 36:7 (ESV)**

**I am thankful for…**

1)________________________________

2)________________________________

3)________________________________

**Scripture Reflection**

________________________________

________________________________

________________________________

**Affirmation — I am…**

________________________________

________________________________

________________________________

**Personal Notes**

________________________________

________________________________

________________________________

________________________________

________________________________

________________________________

________________________________

________________________________

*"There is no more lovely, friendly, and charming relationship, communion or company than a good marriage."*

**Martin Luther**

**Quote Reflection**

______________________________

______________________________

______________________________

**Today was a great day because…**

1)______________________________

2)______________________________

3)______________________________

**I could have made today better by…**

______________________________

______________________________

______________________________

**Personal Notes**

______________________________

______________________________

______________________________

______________________________

______________________________

______________________________

______________________________

______________________________

Date: ____/____/____

*For the Lord disciplines the one he loves,*
*and chastises every son whom he receives.*
**Ephesians 5:33 (ESV)**

**I am thankful for…**

1) ____________________
2) ____________________
3) ____________________

**Scripture Reflection**

____________________
____________________
____________________

**Affirmation — I am…**

____________________
____________________
____________________

**Personal Notes**

____________________
____________________
____________________
____________________
____________________
____________________
____________________
____________________

*"Those privileged to touch the lives of children should constantly be aware that their impact on a single child may affect a multitude of others a thousand years from now."*
**Unknown**

## Quote Reflection

___

___

___

## Today was a great day because…

1)___

2)___

3)___

## I could have made today better by…

___

___

___

## Personal Notes

___

___

___

___

___

___

___

___

Date: ____/____/____

*But when the fullness of time had come, God sent forth his Son, born of woman, born under the law…*
**Galatians 4:4 (ESV)**

## I am thankful for…

1)____________________
2)____________________
3)____________________

## Scripture Reflection

____________________
____________________
____________________

## Affirmation — I am…

____________________
____________________
____________________

## Personal Notes

____________________
____________________
____________________
____________________
____________________
____________________
____________________
____________________

*"It's not only children who grow. Parents do, too.*
*As much as we watch to see what our children do with*
*their lives, they are watching us to see what we do with ours.*
*I can't tell my children to reach for the sun.*
*All I can do is reach for it, myself."*

**Joyce Maynard**

## Quote Reflection

________________________________________

________________________________________

________________________________________

## Today was a great day because…

**1)**______________________________________

**2)**______________________________________

**3)**______________________________________

## I could have made today better by…

________________________________________

________________________________________

________________________________________

## Personal Notes

________________________________________

________________________________________

________________________________________

________________________________________

________________________________________

________________________________________

________________________________________

________________________________________

Date: ____/____/____

*Hear, my son, and accept my words, that the years of your life may be many. I have taught you the way of wisdom; I have led you in the paths of uprightness.*

**Proverbs 4:10-11 (ESV)**

**I am thankful for…**

**1)**______________________________

**2)**______________________________

**3)**______________________________

**Scripture Reflection**

______________________________

______________________________

______________________________

**Affirmation — I am…**

______________________________

______________________________

______________________________

**Personal Notes**

______________________________

______________________________

______________________________

______________________________

______________________________

______________________________

______________________________

______________________________

*"Grandparents are a delightful blend of laughter, caring deeds, wonderful stories and love. "*

**Unknown**

## Quote Reflection

______________________________________________

______________________________________________

______________________________________________

## Today was a great day because…

1)____________________________________________

2)____________________________________________

3)____________________________________________

## I could have made today better by…

______________________________________________

______________________________________________

______________________________________________

## Personal Notes

______________________________________________

______________________________________________

______________________________________________

______________________________________________

______________________________________________

______________________________________________

______________________________________________

______________________________________________

Date: ____/____/________

*The soul who sins shall die.*
*The son shall not suffer for the iniquity of the father,*
*nor the father suffer for the iniquity of the son.*
*The righteousness of the righteous shall be upon himself,*
*and the wickedness of the wicked shall be upon himself.*
**Ezekiel 18:20 (ESV)**

**I am thankful for…**

1)______________________________

2)______________________________

3)______________________________

**Scripture Reflection**

______________________________

______________________________

______________________________

**Affirmation — I am…**

______________________________

______________________________

______________________________

**Personal Notes**

______________________________

______________________________

______________________________

______________________________

______________________________

______________________________

______________________________

______________________________

*"If you are too busy to spend time with your children then you are busier than God intended you to be."*
**Rabbi Mendel Epstein**

## Quote Reflection

______________________________________________

______________________________________________

______________________________________________

## Today was a great day because…

1)____________________________________________

2)____________________________________________

3)____________________________________________

## I could have made today better by…

______________________________________________

______________________________________________

______________________________________________

## Personal Notes

______________________________________________

______________________________________________

______________________________________________

______________________________________________

______________________________________________

______________________________________________

______________________________________________

______________________________________________

Date: ____/____/____

*The father of the righteous will greatly rejoice;*
*he who fathers a wise son will be glad in him.*
**Proverbs 23:24 (ESV)**

**I am thankful for…**

**1)**___________________________

**2)**___________________________

**3)**___________________________

**Scripture Reflection**

___________________________

___________________________

___________________________

**Affirmation — I am…**

___________________________

___________________________

___________________________

**Personal Notes**

___________________________

___________________________

___________________________

___________________________

___________________________

___________________________

___________________________

___________________________

*"Live so that when your children think of fairness and integrity, they think of you."*
**H. Jackson Brown, Jr.**

**Quote Reflection**

______________________________

______________________________

______________________________

**Today was a great day because…**

1)______________________________

2)______________________________

3)______________________________

**I could have made today better by…**

______________________________

______________________________

______________________________

**Personal Notes**

______________________________

______________________________

______________________________

______________________________

______________________________

______________________________

______________________________

______________________________

Date: ____/____/____

*But as for you, continue in what you have learned and have firmly believed, knowing from whom you learned it and how from childhood you have been acquainted with the sacred writings, which are able to make you wise for salvation through faith in Christ Jesus.*

**2 Timothy 3:14-15 (ESV)**

## I am thankful for…

1)____________________

2)____________________

3)____________________

## Scripture Reflection

____________________

____________________

____________________

## Affirmation — I am…

____________________

____________________

____________________

## Personal Notes

____________________

____________________

____________________

____________________

____________________

____________________

____________________

____________________

*"A child enters your home and for the next twenty years makes so much noise you can hardly stand it. The child departs, leaving the house so silent you think you are going mad."*

**John Andrew Holmes**

## Quote Reflection

________________________________________

________________________________________

________________________________________

## Today was a great day because…

**1)**______________________________________

**2)**______________________________________

**3)**______________________________________

## I could have made today better by…

________________________________________

________________________________________

________________________________________

## Personal Notes

________________________________________

________________________________________

________________________________________

________________________________________

________________________________________

________________________________________

________________________________________

________________________________________

Date: ____/____/____

*Behold, I was brought forth in iniquity,*
*and in sin did my mother conceive me.*
**Psalm 51:5 (ESV)**

**I am thankful for…**

1)______________________________

2)______________________________

3)______________________________

**Scripture Reflection**

**Affirmation — I am…**

**Personal Notes**

*"Often the only thing a child can remember about an adult in later years, when he or she is grown, is whether or not that person was kind to him or her."*

**Billy Graham**

## Quote Reflection

______________________________

______________________________

______________________________

## Today was a great day because…

1)______________________________

2)______________________________

3)______________________________

## I could have made today better by…

______________________________

______________________________

______________________________

## Personal Notes

______________________________

______________________________

______________________________

______________________________

______________________________

______________________________

______________________________

______________________________

Date: ____/____/________

*He called a little child to him, and placed the child among them. And he said: "Truly I tell you, unless you change and become like little children, you will never enter the kingdom of heaven. Therefore, whoever takes the lowly position of this child is the greatest in the kingdom of heaven. And whoever welcomes one such child in my name welcomes me.*

**Matthew 18:2-5 (NIV)**

## I am thankful for…

1) ____________________

2) ____________________

3) ____________________

## Scripture Reflection

____________________

____________________

____________________

## Affirmation — I am…

____________________

____________________

____________________

## Personal Notes

____________________

____________________

____________________

____________________

____________________

____________________

____________________

____________________

*"Once we figured out that we could not change each other, we became free to celebrate ourselves as we are."*

**H. Dean Rutherford**

## Quote Reflection

______________________________________________

______________________________________________

______________________________________________

## Today was a great day because…

1)____________________________________________

2)____________________________________________

3)____________________________________________

## I could have made today better by…

______________________________________________

______________________________________________

______________________________________________

## Personal Notes

______________________________________________

______________________________________________

______________________________________________

______________________________________________

______________________________________________

______________________________________________

______________________________________________

______________________________________________

Date: ____/____/____

*Do not be unequally yoked with unbelievers.*
*For what partnership has righteousness with lawlessness?*
*Or what fellowship has light with darkness?*
**2 Corinthians 6:14 (ESV)**

**I am thankful for…**

1)____________________

2)____________________

3)____________________

**Scripture Reflection**

____________________

____________________

____________________

**Affirmation — I am…**

____________________

____________________

____________________

**Personal Notes**

____________________

____________________

____________________

____________________

____________________

____________________

____________________

____________________

*"Some of the world's best educators are grandparents."*
**Dr. Charlie W. Shedd**

**Quote Reflection**

______________________________________________

______________________________________________

______________________________________________

**Today was a great day because…**

1)____________________________________________

2)____________________________________________

3)____________________________________________

**I could have made today better by…**

______________________________________________

______________________________________________

______________________________________________

**Personal Notes**

______________________________________________

______________________________________________

______________________________________________

______________________________________________

______________________________________________

______________________________________________

______________________________________________

______________________________________________

Date: ____/____/____

*Whoever spares the rod hates his son,*
*but he who loves him is diligent to discipline him.*
**Proverbs 13:24 (ESV)**

**I am thankful for…**

1)______________________________
2)______________________________
3)______________________________

**Scripture Reflection**

______________________________
______________________________
______________________________

**Affirmation — I am…**

______________________________
______________________________
______________________________

**Personal Notes**

______________________________
______________________________
______________________________
______________________________
______________________________
______________________________
______________________________
______________________________

*"Listen earnestly to anything your children want to tell you, no matter what. If you don't listen eagerly to the little stuff when they are little, they won't tell you the big stuff when they are big, because to them all of it has always been big stuff."*

**Catherine M. Wallace**

## Quote Reflection

______________________________________________

______________________________________________

______________________________________________

## Today was a great day because…

1)____________________________________________

2)____________________________________________

3)____________________________________________

## I could have made today better by…

______________________________________________

______________________________________________

______________________________________________

## Personal Notes

______________________________________________

______________________________________________

______________________________________________

______________________________________________

______________________________________________

______________________________________________

______________________________________________

______________________________________________

Date: ____/____/____

*So we have come to know and to believe the love that God has for us. God is love, and whoever abides in love abides in God, and God abides in him.*

**1 John 4:16 (ESV)**

**I am thankful for…**

**1)**______________________________

**2)**______________________________

**3)**______________________________

**Scripture Reflection**

______________________________

______________________________

______________________________

**Affirmation — I am…**

______________________________

______________________________

______________________________

**Personal Notes**

______________________________

______________________________

______________________________

______________________________

______________________________

______________________________

______________________________

______________________________

*"There is nothing more wonderful than the love and guidance a grandparent can give his or her grandchild."*
**Edward Fays**

**Quote Reflection**

______________________________

______________________________

______________________________

**Today was a great day because…**

1)______________________________

2)______________________________

3)______________________________

**I could have made today better by…**

______________________________

______________________________

______________________________

**Personal Notes**

______________________________

______________________________

______________________________

______________________________

______________________________

______________________________

______________________________

______________________________

Date: ______/______/__________

*And he said, "Abba, Father, all things are possible for you. Remove this cup from me. Yet not what I will, but what you will."*

**Mark 14:36 (ESV)**

**I am thankful for…**

1)______________________________

2)______________________________

3)______________________________

**Scripture Reflection**

______________________________

______________________________

______________________________

**Affirmation — I am…**

______________________________

______________________________

______________________________

**Personal Notes**

______________________________

______________________________

______________________________

______________________________

______________________________

______________________________

______________________________

______________________________

*"A long-lasting marriage is built by two people who believe in — and live by — the solemn promise they made."*

**Darlene Schacht**

## Quote Reflection

______________________________________________

______________________________________________

______________________________________________

## Today was a great day because…

1)____________________________________________

2)____________________________________________

3)____________________________________________

## I could have made today better by…

______________________________________________

______________________________________________

______________________________________________

## Personal Notes

______________________________________________

______________________________________________

______________________________________________

______________________________________________

______________________________________________

______________________________________________

______________________________________________

______________________________________________

"Finish: Give Yourself the Gift of Done."

Jon Acuff

Again, you are awesome!

I would love to hear of your experience with the journal. How have your journaling efforts changed your family relationships? Shoot me an email at feedback@MichaelTanner.org.

You have about 20 days left in this journal, but don't stop there. Continue building your family legacy by ordering another copy of the journal at MichaelTanner.org/journal.

Journal on!

Date: ____/____/____

*Let deacons each be the husband of one wife,*
*managing their children and their own households well.*
**1 Timothy 3:12 (ESV)**

**I am thankful for…**

1)____________________

2)____________________

3)____________________

**Scripture Reflection**

**Affirmation — I am…**

**Personal Notes**

*"If there is anything that we wish to change in the child, we should first examine it and see whether it is not something that could better be changed in ourselves."*

**Carl Jung**

**Quote Reflection**

________________________________________

________________________________________

________________________________________

**Today was a great day because…**

**1)**______________________________________

**2)**______________________________________

**3)**______________________________________

**I could have made today better by…**

________________________________________

________________________________________

________________________________________

**Personal Notes**

________________________________________

________________________________________

________________________________________

________________________________________

________________________________________

________________________________________

________________________________________

________________________________________

Date: ____/____/____

*She looks well to the ways of her household and does not eat the bread of idleness.*

**Proverbs 31:27 (ESV)**

## I am thankful for…

1) ______________________________

2) ______________________________

3) ______________________________

## Scripture Reflection

______________________________

______________________________

______________________________

## Affirmation — I am…

______________________________

______________________________

______________________________

## Personal Notes

______________________________

______________________________

______________________________

______________________________

______________________________

______________________________

______________________________

______________________________

*"The difference between an ordinary marriage and an extraordinary marriage is in giving just a little 'extra' every day, as often as possible, for as long as we both shall live."*

**Fawn Weaver**

## Quote Reflection

______________________________________________

______________________________________________

______________________________________________

## Today was a great day because…

1)____________________________________________

2)____________________________________________

3)____________________________________________

## I could have made today better by…

______________________________________________

______________________________________________

______________________________________________

## Personal Notes

______________________________________________

______________________________________________

______________________________________________

______________________________________________

______________________________________________

______________________________________________

______________________________________________

______________________________________________

Date: ____/____/____

*A continual dripping on a rainy day*
*and a quarrelsome wife are alike…*
**Proverbs 27:15 (ESV)**

**I am thankful for…**

1)____________________
2)____________________
3)____________________

**Scripture Reflection**

____________________
____________________
____________________

**Affirmation — I am…**

____________________
____________________
____________________

**Personal Notes**

____________________
____________________
____________________
____________________
____________________
____________________
____________________
____________________

*"The history of our grandparents is remembered not with rose petals but in the laughter and tears of their children and their children's children. It is into us that the lives of grandparents have gone. It is in us that their history becomes a future."*

**Charles Morse**

**Quote Reflection**

______________________________________________

______________________________________________

______________________________________________

**Today was a great day because…**

1)____________________________________________

2)____________________________________________

3)____________________________________________

**I could have made today better by…**

______________________________________________

______________________________________________

______________________________________________

**Personal Notes**

______________________________________________

______________________________________________

______________________________________________

______________________________________________

______________________________________________

______________________________________________

______________________________________________

______________________________________________

Date: ____/____/____

*If you, then, though you are evil, know how to give good gifts to your children, how much more will your Father in heaven give good gifts to those who ask him!*

**Matthew 7:11 (NIV)**

## I am thankful for…

1) ________________________________________

2) ________________________________________

3) ________________________________________

## Scripture Reflection

## Affirmation — I am…

## Personal Notes

*"The greatest marriages are built on teamwork.
A mutual respect, a healthy dose of admiration, and a
never-ending portion of love and grace."*
**Fawn Weaver**

## Quote Reflection

______________________________________________

______________________________________________

______________________________________________

## Today was a great day because…

1)____________________________________________

2)____________________________________________

3)____________________________________________

## I could have made today better by…

______________________________________________

______________________________________________

______________________________________________

## Personal Notes

______________________________________________

______________________________________________

______________________________________________

______________________________________________

______________________________________________

______________________________________________

______________________________________________

______________________________________________

Date: ____/____/____

*Like a gold ring in a pig's snout*
*is a beautiful woman without discretion.*
**Proverbs 11:22 (ESV)**

**I am thankful for…**

1)____________________
2)____________________
3)____________________

**Scripture Reflection**

____________________
____________________
____________________

**Affirmation — I am…**

____________________
____________________
____________________

**Personal Notes**

____________________
____________________
____________________
____________________
____________________
____________________
____________________
____________________

*"Other things may change us, but we start and end with the family."*
**Anthony Brandt**

## Quote Reflection

______________________________________________

______________________________________________

______________________________________________

## Today was a great day because…

1)____________________________________________

2)____________________________________________

3)____________________________________________

## I could have made today better by…

______________________________________________

______________________________________________

______________________________________________

## Personal Notes

______________________________________________

______________________________________________

______________________________________________

______________________________________________

______________________________________________

______________________________________________

______________________________________________

______________________________________________

Date: ____/____/____

*Do not be like them, for your Father knows what you need before you ask him.*
**Matthew 6:8 (NIV)**

**I am thankful for…**

1) ____________________
2) ____________________
3) ____________________

**Scripture Reflection**

____________________
____________________
____________________

**Affirmation — I am…**

____________________
____________________
____________________

**Personal Notes**

____________________
____________________
____________________
____________________
____________________
____________________
____________________
____________________

*"Grandparents should play the same role in the family as an elder statesman can in the government of a country. They have the experience and knowledge that comes from surviving a great many years of life's battles and the wisdom, hopefully, to recognize how their grandchildren can benefit from this."*

**Geoff Dench**

## Quote Reflection

______________________________

______________________________

______________________________

## Today was a great day because…

1)______________________________

2)______________________________

3)______________________________

## I could have made today better by…

______________________________

______________________________

______________________________

## Personal Notes

______________________________

______________________________

______________________________

______________________________

______________________________

______________________________

______________________________

______________________________

Date: ____/____/____

*And, "I will be a Father to you, and you will be my sons and daughters, says the Lord Almighty."*
**2 Corinthians 6:18 (NIV)**

**I am thankful for…**

**1)**____________________

**2)**____________________

**3)**____________________

**Scripture Reflection**

____________________

____________________

____________________

**Affirmation — I am…**

____________________

____________________

____________________

**Personal Notes**

____________________

____________________

____________________

____________________

____________________

____________________

____________________

____________________

*"My father didn't tell me how to live;*
*he lived, and let me watch him do it."*
**Clarence Kelland**

## Quote Reflection

______________________________________________
______________________________________________
______________________________________________

## Today was a great day because…

1)____________________________________________
2)____________________________________________
3)____________________________________________

## I could have made today better by…

______________________________________________
______________________________________________
______________________________________________

## Personal Notes

______________________________________________
______________________________________________
______________________________________________
______________________________________________
______________________________________________
______________________________________________
______________________________________________
______________________________________________

Date: ____/____/____

*Then God said, "Let us make man in our image, after our likeness. And let them have dominion over the fish of the sea and over the birds of the heavens and over the livestock and over all the earth and over every creeping thing that creeps on the earth." So God created man in his own image, in the image of God he created him; male and female he created them.*

**Genesis 1:26-27 (ESV)**

## I am thankful for…

**1)**____________________

**2)**____________________

**3)**____________________

## Scripture Reflection

## Affirmation — I am…

## Personal Notes

*"In family life, love is the oil that eases friction, the cement that binds closer together, and the music that brings harmony."*

**Friedrich Nietzsche**

## Quote Reflection

______________________________

______________________________

______________________________

## Today was a great day because…

1)______________________________

2)______________________________

3)______________________________

## I could have made today better by…

______________________________

______________________________

______________________________

## Personal Notes

______________________________

______________________________

______________________________

______________________________

______________________________

______________________________

______________________________

______________________________

Date: ____/____/____

*He heals the brokenhearted and binds up their wounds.*

**Psalm 147:3 (ESV)**

**I am thankful for…**

1) ____________________

2) ____________________

3) ____________________

**Scripture Reflection**

____________________

____________________

____________________

**Affirmation — I am…**

____________________

____________________

____________________

**Personal Notes**

____________________

____________________

____________________

____________________

____________________

____________________

____________________

____________________

*"When people tell me they've learned from experience,*
*I tell them the trick is to learn from other people's experience."*
**Warren Buffett**

## Quote Reflection

______________________________________________

______________________________________________

______________________________________________

## Today was a great day because…

1)____________________________________________

2)____________________________________________

3)____________________________________________

## I could have made today better by…

______________________________________________

______________________________________________

______________________________________________

## Personal Notes

______________________________________________

______________________________________________

______________________________________________

______________________________________________

______________________________________________

______________________________________________

______________________________________________

______________________________________________

Date: ____/____/________

*Do all things without grumbling or disputing, that you may be blameless and innocent, children of God without blemish in the midst of a crooked and twisted generation, among whom you shine as lights in the world, holding fast to the word of life, so that in the day of Christ I may be proud that I did not run in vain or labor in vain.*

**Philippians 2:14-16 (ESV)**

**I am thankful for…**

**1)**________________________________

**2)**________________________________

**3)**________________________________

**Scripture Reflection**

________________________________

________________________________

________________________________

**Affirmation — I am…**

________________________________

________________________________

________________________________

**Personal Notes**

________________________________

________________________________

________________________________

________________________________

________________________________

________________________________

________________________________

________________________________

*"There really are places in the heart you don't even know exist until you love a child."*

**Anne Lamott**

## Quote Reflection

________________________________________

________________________________________

________________________________________

## Today was a great day because…

**1)**______________________________________

**2)**______________________________________

**3)**______________________________________

## I could have made today better by…

________________________________________

________________________________________

________________________________________

## Personal Notes

________________________________________

________________________________________

________________________________________

________________________________________

________________________________________

________________________________________

________________________________________

________________________________________

Date: ____/____/____

*Behold, I have engraved you on the palms of my hands;*
*your walls are continually before me.*
**Isaiah 49:16 (ESV)**

**I am thankful for…**

1) ______________________________

2) ______________________________

3) ______________________________

**Scripture Reflection**

______________________________

______________________________

______________________________

**Affirmation — I am…**

______________________________

______________________________

______________________________

**Personal Notes**

______________________________

______________________________

______________________________

______________________________

______________________________

______________________________

______________________________

______________________________

*"Marriage has the power to set the course of your life as a whole. If your marriage is strong, even if all the circumstances in your life around you are filled with trouble and weakness, it won't matter. You will be able to move out into the world in strength."*

**Timothy Keller**

## Quote Reflection

________________________________________

________________________________________

________________________________________

## Today was a great day because…

**1)**______________________________________

**2)**______________________________________

**3)**______________________________________

## I could have made today better by…

________________________________________

________________________________________

________________________________________

## Personal Notes

________________________________________

________________________________________

________________________________________

________________________________________

________________________________________

________________________________________

________________________________________

________________________________________

Date: ____/____/____

*For by grace you have been saved through faith.*
*And this is not your own doing; it is the gift of God,*
**Ephesians 2:8 (ESV)**

**I am thankful for…**

1)______________________________
2)______________________________
3)______________________________

**Scripture Reflection**

______________________________
______________________________
______________________________

**Affirmation — I am…**

______________________________
______________________________
______________________________

**Personal Notes**

______________________________
______________________________
______________________________
______________________________
______________________________
______________________________
______________________________
______________________________

*"Marriages, like a garden, take time to grow. But the harvest is rich unto those who patiently and tenderly care for the ground."*
**Darlene Schacht**

## Quote Reflection

______________________________________________

______________________________________________

______________________________________________

## Today was a great day because…

**1)**______________________________________________

**2)**______________________________________________

**3)**______________________________________________

## I could have made today better by…

______________________________________________

______________________________________________

______________________________________________

## Personal Notes

______________________________________________

______________________________________________

______________________________________________

______________________________________________

______________________________________________

______________________________________________

______________________________________________

______________________________________________

Date: ______/______/______

*I praise you, for I am fearfully and wonderfully made.*
*Wonderful are your works; my soul knows it very well.*
**Psalm 139:14 (ESV)**

**I am thankful for…**

1)____________________
2)____________________
3)____________________

**Scripture Reflection**

____________________
____________________
____________________

**Affirmation — I am…**

____________________
____________________
____________________

**Personal Notes**

____________________
____________________
____________________
____________________
____________________
____________________
____________________
____________________

*"The greatest favor we can do our children is to give visible example of love and esteem to our spouse. As they grow up, they may then look forward to maturity so they too can find such love."*
**Eucharista Ward**

## Quote Reflection

______________________________________________

______________________________________________

______________________________________________

## Today was a great day because…

**1)**____________________________________________

**2)**____________________________________________

**3)**____________________________________________

## I could have made today better by…

______________________________________________

______________________________________________

______________________________________________

## Personal Notes

______________________________________________

______________________________________________

______________________________________________

______________________________________________

______________________________________________

______________________________________________

______________________________________________

______________________________________________

Date: ____/____/____

*We love because he first loved us.*
**1 John 4:19 (ESV)**

**I am thankful for…**

1)____________________

2)____________________

3)____________________

**Scripture Reflection**

____________________

____________________

____________________

**Affirmation — I am…**

____________________

____________________

____________________

**Personal Notes**

____________________

____________________

____________________

____________________

____________________

____________________

____________________

____________________

*"Your priorities aren't what you SAY they are. They are revealed by how you live. What does your life say about the value of your family and marriage?"*

**Jimmy Evans**

## Quote Reflection

______________________________

______________________________

______________________________

## Today was a great day because…

**1)**______________________________

**2)**______________________________

**3)**______________________________

## I could have made today better by…

______________________________

______________________________

______________________________

## Personal Notes

______________________________

______________________________

______________________________

______________________________

______________________________

______________________________

______________________________

______________________________

Date: _____/_____/_____

*As a father shows compassion to his children,*
*so the Lord shows compassion to those who fear him.*
**Psalm 103:13 (ESV)**

**I am thankful for…**

1)________________________________________
2)________________________________________
3)________________________________________

**Scripture Reflection**

________________________________________
________________________________________
________________________________________

**Affirmation — I am…**

________________________________________
________________________________________
________________________________________

**Personal Notes**

________________________________________
________________________________________
________________________________________
________________________________________
________________________________________
________________________________________
________________________________________
________________________________________

*"What a wonderful contribution our grandmothers and grandfathers can make if they will share some of the rich experiences and their testimonies with their children and grandchildren."*
**Vaughn J. Featherstone**

**Quote Reflection**

________________________________________

________________________________________

________________________________________

**Today was a great day because…**

**1)**______________________________________

**2)**______________________________________

**3)**______________________________________

**I could have made today better by…**

________________________________________

________________________________________

________________________________________

**Personal Notes**

________________________________________

________________________________________

________________________________________

________________________________________

________________________________________

________________________________________

________________________________________

________________________________________

Date: ______/______/______

*The steadfast love of the Lord never ceases; his mercies never come to an end; they are new every morning; great is your faithfulness.*
**Lamentations 3:22-23 (ESV)**

**I am thankful for…**

1) ______________________________
2) ______________________________
3) ______________________________

**Scripture Reflection**

______________________________
______________________________
______________________________

**Affirmation — I am…**

______________________________
______________________________
______________________________

**Personal Notes**

______________________________
______________________________
______________________________
______________________________
______________________________
______________________________
______________________________
______________________________

*"We never know the love of the parent*
*till we become parents ourselves."*
**Henry Ward Beecher**

## Quote Reflection

______________________________

______________________________

______________________________

## Today was a great day because…

1)______________________________

2)______________________________

3)______________________________

## I could have made today better by…

______________________________

______________________________

______________________________

## Personal Notes

______________________________

______________________________

______________________________

______________________________

______________________________

______________________________

______________________________

______________________________

Date: ____/____/____

*But to all who did receive him, who believed in his name,*
*he gave the right to become children of God...*
**John 1:12 (ESV)**

## I am thankful for...

1) ____________________

2) ____________________

3) ____________________

## Scripture Reflection

____________________

____________________

____________________

## Affirmation — I am...

____________________

____________________

____________________

## Personal Notes

____________________

____________________

____________________

____________________

____________________

____________________

____________________

____________________

*"Happy is the man who finds a true friend, and far happier is he who finds that true friend in his wife."*
**Franz Schubert**

## Quote Reflection

______________________________________________

______________________________________________

______________________________________________

## Today was a great day because…

1)____________________________________________

2)____________________________________________

3)____________________________________________

## I could have made today better by…

______________________________________________

______________________________________________

______________________________________________

## Personal Notes

______________________________________________

______________________________________________

______________________________________________

______________________________________________

______________________________________________

______________________________________________

______________________________________________

______________________________________________

Date: ____/____/____

*Keep your life free from love of money, and be content with what you have, for he has said, "I will never leave you nor forsake you."*
**Hebrews 13:5 (ESV)**

**I am thankful for…**

1) ____________________
2) ____________________
3) ____________________

**Scripture Reflection**

____________________
____________________
____________________

**Affirmation — I am…**

____________________
____________________
____________________

**Personal Notes**

____________________
____________________
____________________
____________________
____________________
____________________
____________________
____________________

*"Friendship in marriage is the spark that lights an everlasting flame."*
**Fawn Weaver**

## Quote Reflection

______________________________
______________________________
______________________________

## Today was a great day because…

1)______________________________
2)______________________________
3)______________________________

## I could have made today better by…

______________________________
______________________________
______________________________

## Personal Notes

______________________________
______________________________
______________________________
______________________________
______________________________
______________________________
______________________________
______________________________

Date: ____/____/____

*For the mountains may depart and the hills be removed, but my steadfast love shall not depart from you, and my covenant of peace shall not be removed," says the Lord, who has compassion on you.*

**Isaiah 54:10 (ESV)**

**I am thankful for…**

1)______________________________

2)______________________________

3)______________________________

**Scripture Reflection**

______________________________

______________________________

______________________________

**Affirmation — I am…**

______________________________

______________________________

______________________________

**Personal Notes**

______________________________

______________________________

______________________________

______________________________

______________________________

______________________________

______________________________

______________________________

*"Life affords no greater responsibility, no greater privilege, than the raising of the next generation."*
**C. Everett Koop**

**Quote Reflection**

______________________________

______________________________

______________________________

**Today was a great day because…**

1)______________________________

2)______________________________

3)______________________________

**I could have made today better by…**

______________________________

______________________________

______________________________

**Personal Notes**

______________________________

______________________________

______________________________

______________________________

______________________________

______________________________

______________________________

______________________________

Date: ____/____/____

*All we like sheep have gone astray; we have turned — every one — to his own way; and the Lord has laid on him the iniquity of us all.*
**Isaiah 53:6 (ESV)**

**I am thankful for…**

1)____________________

2)____________________

3)____________________

**Scripture Reflection**

**Affirmation — I am…**

**Personal Notes**

*"When there is love in a marriage, there is harmony in the home; when there is harmony in the home, there is contentment in the community; when there is contentment in the community, there is prosperity in the nation; when there is prosperity in the nation, there is peace in the world."*

**Chinese Proverb**

## Quote Reflection

______________________________

______________________________

______________________________

## Today was a great day because…

1)______________________________

2)______________________________

3)______________________________

## I could have made today better by…

______________________________

______________________________

______________________________

## Personal Notes

______________________________

______________________________

______________________________

______________________________

______________________________

______________________________

______________________________

______________________________

# About the Author

Michael Tanner has a M.A. in Christian Leadership from Luther Rice College & Seminary. With twenty-three years of marriage and parenting three teenagers under their belt, Michael and his wife Jennifer have experienced the highs and lows of marriage and the challenges of parenting in today's world. Michael shares this education and experience with readers and listeners at http://MichaelTanner.org in order to offer real help and hope to every family.

# Endnotes

i. http://www.nationalreview.com/article/425957/family-structure-matters-science-proves-it-w-bradford-wilcox

ii. http://www.health.harvard.edu/newsletter_article/in-praise-of-gratitude

iii. https://www.psychologicalscience.org/news/releases/rest-is-not-idleness-reflection-is-critical-for-development-and-well-being.html#.WVuY28aZOu4

iv. https://academic.oup.com/scan/article/11/4/621/2375054/Self-affirmation-activates-brain-systems

v. http://www.businessinsider.com/sleep-science-patrick-fuller-harvard-good-snooze-2016-2/#he-sets-the-sleeping-mood-5

ESV—Scripture marked ESV is taken from the *ESV Study Bible*. English Standard Version, Crossway, 2008.

*NIV*—Scripture marked NIV is taken from the *Holy Bible*. New International Version, Biblica, 2011.

*HCSB*—Scripture marked HCSB is taken from the *Holy Bible*. Holman Christian Standard Bible, Holman Bible Publishers, 2003.

*NKJV*—Scripture marked NKJV is taken from the *Holy Bible*. New King James Version, Thomas Nelson,1982.

www.TheMorganJamesSpeakersGroup.com

We connect Morgan James published authors with live and online events and audiences who will benefit from their expertise.

Printed in the USA
CPSIA information can be obtained
at www.ICGtesting.com
JSHW022211140824
68134JS00018B/992